T0163036

Kitchen Witchcraft: The Element of Earth

The fourth book in the Kitchen Witchcraft series
along with *Spells & Charms*, *Garden Magic* and
Crystal Magic

Kitchen Witchcraft: The Element of Earth

The fourth book in the Kitchen Witchcraft series along with *Spells & Charms, Garden Magic* and *Crystal Magic*

Rachel Patterson

MOON BOOKS

Winchester, UK
Washington, USA

JOHN HUNT PUBLISHING

First published by Moon Books, 2021
Moon Books is an imprint of John Hunt Publishing Ltd., No. 3 East Street, Alresford
Hampshire SO24 9EE, UK
office@jhpbooks.net
www.johnhuntpublishing.com
www.moon-books.net

For distributor details and how to order please visit the 'Ordering' section on our website.

Text copyright: Rachel Patterson 2020

ISBN: 978 1 78904 349 5
978 1 78904 350 1 (ebook)
Library of Congress Control Number: 2020931759

A CIP catalogue record for this book is available from the British Library.

Design: Stuart Davies

UK: Printed and bound by CPI Group (UK) Ltd, Croydon, CR0 4YY
US: Printed and bound by Thomson-Shore, 7300 West Joy Road, Dexter, MI 48130

We operate a distinctive and ethical publishing philosophy in
all areas of our business, from our global network of authors to
production and worldwide distribution.

Contents

Also by Rachel Patterson

Kitchen Witchcraft Series
Spells & Charms
Garden Magic
Crystal Magic

Pagan Portals
Kitchen Witchcraft
Hoodoo Folk Magic
Moon Magic
Meditation
The Cailleach
Animal Magic
Sun Magic

Other Books
The Art of Ritual
Witchcraft ... into the Wilds
Grimoire of a Kitchen Witch
A Kitchen Witch's World of Magical Foods
A Kitchen Witch's World of Magical Plants & Herbs
Arc of the Goddess (co-written with Tracey Roberts)
Moon Books Gods & Goddesses Colouring Book (Patterson family)
Practically Pagan: Cooking

Who am I?

I am a witch ... and have been for a very long time. I am also a working wife and mother who has also been lucky enough to write and have published a book or fifteen. I love to learn, I love to study and have done so from books, online resources, schools and wonderful mentors over the years and continue to learn every day but have learnt the most from getting outside and doing it.

I like to laugh, bake and eat cake... I am High Priestess of the Kitchen Witch Coven and an Elder at the online Kitchen Witch School.

My website and personal blog: www.rachelpatterson.co.uk
Facebook: www.facebook.com/rachelpattersonbooks
Email: kitchenwitchhearth@yahoo.com
Kitchen Witch School website and blog:
www.kitchenwitchhearth.net
www.facebook.com/kitchenwitchuk

I also have regular blogs on:
Witches & Pagans - www.witchesandpagans.com/pagan-paths-blogs/hedge-witch.html
Patheos Pagan - www.patheos.com/blogs/beneaththemoon
Moon Books - www.johnhuntpublishing.com/moon-books/

My craft is a combination of old religion Witchcraft, Kitchen Witchery, Hedge Witchery and folk magic.

My heart is that of a Kitchen Witch.

This book will focus on the element of Earth; what it is, the correspondences, how to work with it, earth elementals, meditations, rituals and basically everything earth related. Let's get our hands dirty…

Earth beneath me
Sky above me
Air around me
Mother earth to ground me

Earth: The basics

The elements are the original foundation of which all other things are made, by unification or transformation. The ancients divided the world into four basic elements which we know as Earth, Fire, Air, and Water. These four elements are vital to our survival for without any one of them we could not exist. The four elements, five if you count ether/spirit make up the base foundation of magic. We use them in ritual, energy work, healing and spell work.

We are all probably drawn more to one element than the others. They each have their own unique characteristics and properties that we can tap in to. They can be used individually or mix 'n match to add power.

I do think it helps to have a balance of them all.

We start with earth as this is the element that all of us can relate most to, after all, in many myths the first man was said to be made from earth or clay. Earth *is* nature, it is our mother, and it is our body. We walk upon it every day; we grow our food within its moist soil, and we bury our dead within its silent embrace.

Earth is the element of stability, foundation, strength, growth and prosperity in all its forms. Earth is the densest of all the elements and is physically manifested in stones, rocks, crystals and gems. Earth is a heavy and passive element. It has associations with darkness, thickness and silence. Earth also rules physical things and places, such as the body, nature, chasms, caves, groves, fields, rocks, gems and minerals, standing stones, mountains and metal.

In most traditions of witchcraft, earth is located at the north of the ritual circle and is associated with midnight, the time of silence.

Salt being a very powerful, magical ingredient is also often seen on a witch's altar to represent the element of Earth. Salt used to be a very valuable commodity which was once used as currency. It was also a vital preserving agent to conserve food and prevent starvation through the winter months. Other symbols of Earth which you may find on an altar would be stones and crystals. Here are a few of my own earth correspondences:

Gender – Feminine

Animals – Bear, Boar, Bull, Cattle, Earthworm, Goat, Pigs

Colour – Green, Brown, Black, yellow

Direction – North

Divination – Tarot, Runes, Ogham

Energy – receptive

Time – night

Magic – Burying, Planting, Magnet, Image, Stone, Tree, Knot/ cord, Binding, Garden

Magical Tool – Pentacle

Musical Instrument – Drums and Percussion

Symbols – salt, soil, rocks, stones, leaves, seeds, grasses, twigs, books

Places – Caves, Canyons, Forests, Groves, Valleys, Fields, Farms, Gardens, Parks, Kitchens, Mines, holes, libraries, chasms, garden centres, farmers markets, basements/ cellars, holes, crossroads

Spell work/Rituals/ Positive Qualities – Abundance, Prosperity, Fertility, Grounding, Employment, Stability, endurance, tolerance, patience, planning, career, selfishness, practicality, responsibility, sensuality, strength, tolerance, fertility, wealth, wisdom, potential, reaping, sowing, humility, responsibility, tolerance, practicality

Negatives – depression, domineering, greed, attention seeking, laziness, melancholy, stubbornness

Season – Autumn or Winter (beliefs differ)

Spirits – Gnomes, Dwarfs, Trolls, Leprechauns, Elves, Dryads and Brownies

Zodiac – Capricorn, Taurus and Virgo.
Tarot – Pentacles
Pentagram position – lower left
Archangel – Uriel

The Elemental You

Most of us will find that we are aligned more with one element than another. This may be affected by the zodiac sign we were born under; it may also be because of the work we do or the life we lead. Every mundane task carries a correspondence to one of the elements. The challenge is to create balance in ourselves between all four elements. You might like to make a list to see which element you are heavy in and which ones you might need to work a little more with to bring about balance. Let's look at the everyday element of earth related tasks:

- Gardening
- Charity work
- Working in the greenhouse/visiting a garden centre
- Cooking with herbs and vegetables
- Reading
- Walking the dog
- Recycling
- Housework
- Picking up litter
- Walking
- Visiting sacred/ancient sites
- Going to the library
- These should get you started!

Exercise: Make a list of all your daily chores and activities. Separate them into elements. Which element has the longest list? Which has the shortest? What could you do to help balance your elements out?

Earth Energy

As we work with the positive and negative, sun and moon, masculine and feminine, energy too has opposites. Those of receptive and projective. The flow of energy for the element of earth is receptive.

Receptive energy is also described as being feminine, soothing, passive, spiritual, calming, cold, attracting and magnetic. Receptive energy is good for absorbing negative energy and feelings, but also good for meditation, grounding and psychic abilities.

We can connect with the element of earth in many ways. The obvious ones are practical, by getting our hands dirty in the soil gardening or standing bare foot on the sand or grass. But there are also many magical ways to connect as well (many are suggested within this book), such as working with tree magic or grounding. There are mundane chores that also connect us to the element or earth, I think housework or creating a meal also connect with the element of earth.

Just a reminder…when you work with energy, don't draw it from within yourself. That can be extremely draining and cause you to become very tired or even poorly. Use your body as a channel for the energy. Mother Earth is very happy to lend you the energy you need, all you must do is draw it from her and channel it to where you want it to go.

Earth Magic

Several types of magic lend themselves to working with the earth element.

Burying – perhaps an obvious one. Burying your petitions in soil is perfect. Burying spells at crossroads is also very traditional. Spell remnants can also be buried. Just be mindful to only bury biodegradable items.

Planting – planting seeds as part of spell work features heavily in a lot of magic, particularly in the spring. But it also covers planting of ideas using more mature flora and fauna and trees too.

Magnet – it's all about the attraction! Using magnets to attract something towards you or keeping something, or someone together.

Image – using photos or poppets work really well. These are used to represent the target of your magic.

Stones – using pebbles to absorb your negative vibe and throwing away to remove negative energy both work well. Or using a stone to hold your petition in place whilst the magic works. A petition can also be wrapped and tied around a stone to impart earth energy or keep things held in place.

Tree magic – Trees have their roots deep in the earth which is their connection to the Underworld/Otherworld, their trunks are in the land of men or the Middle World and the top branches reaching up to the sky making the connection to the Upper World. In fact, a tree is an excellent focus point for journeying or as I do, Hedge Riding. The tree is an access point to the three different realms.

There is a huge joke about 'tree huggers' but seriously hugging a tree does you the world of good and it can also lend you energy, healing, knowledge and wisdom. However, don't forget to ask permission first, not all trees want to be hugged and not all trees will be happy to work with you. Ask first and respect the answer you are given. Trees are also our seasonal compass.

Each variety of tree has specific magical properties and you will find on closer inspection that each individual tree has its own unique personality. To discover what each tree means and what magical properties it can or is happy to share with you I suggest meeting each tree and asking.

Knot/cord magic – Long stems of grass really lend themselves to knot magic, but you can also use thin stems of plants such as ivy or even twine, string or ribbon.

If you have the patience you can 'weave' a ball of grass and hang it up in your home to provide protection, you can also plait the longer stems to make witches ladders.

Long stems of grass can also be used for bindings and to control a person's movements, to stop them from causing harm or to tie something down, magically of course not literally...

You can bind pretty much any intent by sealing it with a knot. If you want a new job, a new dress or maybe a holiday, pick your intent and tie the energy into a knot.

Tie a knot with the intent of prosperity, good health and luck and hang it over your front door so that every time someone walks in, they bring the positive energy with them.

If you are crafty you can of course take the knot magic a step further and crochet, weave or knit energy into something beautiful by putting the magic in as you create.

Need to boost your memory or remember something important? Tie a knot in a piece of string and seal it in, when you see the knot you will know that you have to remember something...of course then you have to remember exactly what is it that you need to remember...

Then there is the flip side of binding and knot magic, in that you can undo it too. You can unbind a spell, a curse, an influence or negative energy. You do this simply by binding the intent into the knot and then unravelling it.

Curses and hexes can be bound into knot magic - just say your curse out loud as you tie each knot.

You can keep the knot magic simple by literally just visualising or saying the intent as you tie the knot or you can put on a whole ritual with candles, incense and plinky plonky music, the choice is yours. You can even sprinkle the knot with corresponding herbs or dab with anointing oil.

Binding – this is a form of spell that binds a person or situation so that they/it can no longer harm you. I have found this form of working particularly successful. As long as you are pure in your intent, it doesn't actually harm the person or cause them any discomfort, it just stops them from hurting or harassing you. But bear in mind that this spell does take away the free will of the person you are binding, so use with caution.

A binding spell can be very simple – you use an object that represents the person causing you harm – it can be a poppet; it could be a photograph or it just a lump of clay that you have identified as the person. It can then be bound, with string, ribbon, ivy, or I have found that sticky tape works extremely well. As you bind the object visualise binding the harmful energies of that person and speak your wishes, that the person can no longer harm you or harass you. Bury the spell.

Garden & houseplants – Being in regular contact with your garden and what you grow, even with your house plants or a few pots of herbs, can help you to connect with the spirit of nature and recognise the subtleties of the changing of the seasons and your garden can also provide you with food and magical ingredients. It is also a perfect place to work and leave spells to 'do their thing'. Having that connection also helps you to keep in tune with the turning of the seasons. The garden and plants within give you a direct source of earth elemental energy. You could even design a garden around the element of earth; include lots of stones and pebbles and plants that correspond to the element.

Bottles – witch bottles can be filled with soil, pebbles, flour, rice etc and also buried afterwards. They are essentially a 'spell in a bottle'.

Sigils – symbols and sigils can be drawn on the ground or flat surface using soil or sand. But also painted using soil mixed with water. This also works with ashes from the fire mixed with liquid. Sigils are a personal way of drawing a magical symbol and will be unique to you and each one will be different depending on what you want to bring in. First you need an intent and a phrase that sums up your intended outcome.

Let's look at *"give me strength"*. We will use the letters of the phrase to create the sigil but we need to simplify it first by removing both the vowels and the letters that are duplicated, so once you have done that you end up with: *gvmstrnh*.

Now you need to grab a pen or pencil and paper and draw the letters onto a piece of paper, you can draw them one on top of another or you can space them out linking them together – be guided by your intuition and be as creative or as simple as you want.

Once you have done that your sigil is done and can be used in magical workings, your intent is in the letters, so you can bury it in the earth, burn it in the fire or wash it away in water – whatever works for you.

Time

Another association for the elements is the time of day. Earth links with the night, particularly midnight. What does this mean though? For me, if I am working with the earth element in a spell, I try to work it at night to add an extra layer of power, but it doesn't always fit in with my plans!

Exercise: Work spells at different times and record the results, does it make a difference?

Symbols

Probably the most recognised symbols for the elements are the triangles. Earth is represented by a downward pointing triangle with a line that runs horizontally across. The downward triangle represents the female form and the line shows that it is denser than water (which is represented by a downward triangle without the line).

If you want to represent earth on your altar, in ritual or for spell work there are several items you can use:

Soil – is the obvious one. It is just perfect, but sand can also be used.

Salt – corresponds with earth. It doesn't have to be any fancy kind although you can get all sorts such as pink and black salt. The black salt is usually sea salt mixed with charcoal. Cheap table salt is just fine.

Rocks and pebbles – are totally earthy. Again, it doesn't have to be some exotic pebble from a sacred place, shingle from your garden works.

If you collect a pebble from the beach or river it also has added water energy.

Leaves – from any plant or tree, represent the element of earth.

Twigs – again from any tree or plant, but most definitely earth energy.

Seeds and nuts - although each plant will have its own

element correspondence, I think seeds and nuts in general represent earth.

Roots – couldn't get more earthy, could you?

Books – perhaps slightly random, but books always seem earthy to me, maybe with added air?

Pentagram

The pentagram is a five-pointed star, encased by an outer circle. Its apex points upwards.

The pentagram was first used around 3500BC at Ur of the Chaldees in Ancient Mesopotamia. (No, I personally don't remember that far back). In later Mesopotamian art the pentagram was used as a symbol of imperial power in royal inscriptions. It symbolised the imperial power extending out to the four corners of the world. The Hebrews also used the pentagram as a symbol of truth and for the five books of the Pentateuch (the first five books of the Hebrew scriptures).

The geometry of the pentagram and its metaphysical associations were explored by Pythagoreans who saw it as a symbol of perfection. It was called the Pentalpha, composed of five geometrical 'A's. Pythagoras travelled all over the ancient world. So, he may be the explanation of the presence of the pentagram in Tantrik art, early Hindu and Buddhist writings that seem to share Pythagoras' view of the star.

The Gnostics saw the pentagram as a blazing star, symbolising the crescent moon which related to magic and mysteries of the night time sky and the dark.

Celtic Druids believed the pentagram to be a symbol of the Godhead. Celtic pagans saw the number five as sacred in many things. Examples of this are Ireland having had five great roads, five provinces and five paths of law. Faeries counted by fives and mythological figures wore fivefold cloaks.

It was also a symbol of the underground womb and bears a symbolic relationship to the pyramid forms to the Egyptians.

Even early Christians used the pentagram, it symbolised the five wounds of Christ and up until medieval times it was used as a Christian symbol on occasion. The pentagram implied truth, religious mysticism and the work of the creator. It was only after the Inquisition that the 'evil' associations were assigned to the pentagram. Over time the Christians dropped the use of the circle and just used the five-pointed star.

In Medieval times the pentagram with one point upwards symbolised summer and with two points upwards signified winter. In the legend of Sir Gawain and the Green Knight, the pentagram was his signature glyph and was used on his shield. We are told that this symbolised the five knightly virtues; generosity, courtesy, chastity, chivalry and piety.

The Knights Templar formed during the Crusades used the symbol of the pentagon in their architecture and designs. During the Inquisition the pentagram was seen as a goat's head or the Devil. In the purge on witches, horned gods such as Pan became equated with the Christian's idea of the Devil. And the pentagram, for the first time in history was equated with evil and labelled the Witch's Foot.

During the Renaissance period Hermeticism (the proto science of alchemy) developed along with occult philosophy and symbolism. Graphical and geometric symbols became very important. Western occult teachings began to emphasize the philosophies of man being the small part of the larger universal spirit – "as above, so below". The pentagram returned as the Star of the Microcosm, symbolising man within the macrocosm. In 1582 Tycho Brahe's Calendarium Naturale Magicum Perpetuum shows a pentagram with a body imposed and the Hebrew YHSVH associated with the elements. And we are all familiar with Leonardo da Vinci's drawing of the geometric relationships of man to the universe. Later the pentagram came to be symbolic of the relationship of the head to the four limbs and hence of the pure concentrated essence of anything, such as the spirit, to the four traditional elements.

Masonry uses the pentagram to show man as the smaller aspect of the universe. The pentagram then being incorporated into American symbols. The five-pointed stars on the flag and the eye/pyramid on money.

In the 19th Century we start to see the first modern association of the pentagram with evil – Eliphaz Levi Zahed illustrated the upright pentagram beside an inverted pentagram with the goat's head of Baphomet. This has led to the concept of the different orientations being good and evil. Although, I stress here that in my experience Baphomet has had a raw deal and is definitely not evil...

In the 1940's Gerald Gardner adopted the pentagram with two points upward as the sigil of a second-degree initiation. The one-point upward pentagram together with the upright triangle symbolising third degree initiation. A point downward triangle being the symbol of first-degree initiates.

The pentagram was also inscribed on the altar with its points symbolising the three aspects of the goddess plus the two aspects of the God in a special form of Gardnerian pentacle.

Christians still kept the pentagram as a negative symbol in modern society, so it wasn't until the 1960's that the pentagram was used and worn again in public.

The Church of Satan was an organisation that started out as a practice of following Set, an Egyptian deity. For its emblem they used the inverted pentagram after the Baphomet image of Levi. The reaction of the Christian church was to condemn Satanism as evil and, of course, this lumped all pagan societies together as Devil worship. The stigma of Witchcraft and its use of the pentagram has continued through to today.

Despite the use and the different meaning of the inverted pentagram as a symbol of Gardnerian initiation, modern witchcraft traditions tend to use the upright pentagram. Taoism also uses the pentacle, each point signifying wood, fire, earth, metal and water. The pentacle is the simplest form of star shape that can be drawn unicursally, with a single line, hence it has been called the endless knot.

The pentagram is a symbol of Wiccan and some neopagan spiritual beliefs. The pentagram symbolises the elements of earth, air, water and fire, with the top point representing spirit. It is used in jewellery, on clothing and altars. It is also used in some blessings and healings. The circle around the star represents protection, eternity and infinity. The circle touching all five points indicates that spirit, earth, air, water and fire are all connected.

Invoking and Banishing Pentagrams

You can use a pentagram to invoke or banish the elements in ritual. Each element starts and ends with a different point of the pentagram. The symbols are drawn in the air using your finger, a wand or an athame. As you draw the image, visualise it appearing in the air before you.

To call the element of earth start with your finger/wand/ athame at the top of the pentagram and draw a line down to the left point (earth) first then continue back up to draw the rest of the pentagram. The earth invoking and banishing pentagram are often the most used ones, this one can be used for all invoking and banishing (not just when calling upon the element of earth).

To banish the element of earth, perform the action in reverse, starting from the bottom left point.

To keep silent

In modern Wicca the Witch's Pyramid features the four elements plus that of spirit. It is not actually a physical pyramid, but forms the shape of one. Each point represents one of the elements and this can be reflected in the pentagram shape too. This refers to working magic and ritual and keeping silent about the workings. The thought being that once the magic is worked you don't discuss it so as not to add any interference to the energy. I think it is also about being mindful of how you speak, words have power and can affect others in very strong ways.

Instrument

Ah...the drum. One of my personal favourites. Drums can be all shapes and sizes and made from different materials. I am very honoured to have had the opportunity to birth my own drum a few years ago from a Scottish stag skin. I also have a Bodhran which has a goat skin. You can now also purchase drums with manmade skins.

The sound of the drum is very primal and can send you on a journey or meditation with ease. It is so very definitely earthy. In fact, a lot of the percussion instruments align themselves with the element of earth, tambourines and blocks, for example.

Grounding

If you have been working a lot with energy or you have had a particularly spiritual ritual or experience, you may find yourself feeling a bit lightheaded or even with a headache. This usually means you need to ground. This is important and not just when in ritual, you can ground and centre whenever you need to and in fact it is a useful trick to do during your day.

Energy work can make you feel very floaty and although it is a nice feeling for a while there will be a hard come down afterwards. To avoid that you, can ground yourself. This is a way of connecting with the energy of the earth and releasing any excess energy out from your system.

Grounding involves connecting with the Earth to calm and focus you. You know that totally hyper feeling you get sometimes? It might be after ritual, it might be when you have gotten yourself worked up into a complete hissy fit, and it might be because you have eaten too many marshmallows (ahem). Grounding allows you to drain off that excess energy and re-focus.

Some easy options are to clap your hands and stamp your feet, to eat something such as chocolate or cake (obviously my personal choice). Or you can place your hands palms facing downwards onto the ground and allow the excess energy to drain back into Mother Earth. Take your shoes off and go stand on the grass, the soil or the sand.

Grounding exercise: This is a useful exercise to work with at any time you feel the need to ground:

Sit or stand comfortably and close your eyes.
Visualise roots beginning to grow from the soles of your feet or the base of your spine. As they grow twisting and turning, they plunge down into the lush soil of Mother Earth.
The roots push down deeper into the soil allowing any excess

energy to seep out and into the earth.

If you stretch down far enough your roots will tap into the centre of the earth and you can draw up the balancing, comforting energy back into your body to bring you peace, calm and focus.

When you are ready slowly draw your roots back up through the soil and into your body.

If you are really, seriously hyper I find it helps to visualise your arms stretching up to the sky at well. Feeling your arms, your hands and your fingers becoming branches and sprouting leaves. This can be an exercise where you sit on your yoga mat with incense burning and plinky plonky music to give a really good experience. However, it can also be a seriously quick grounding when you have two minutes to spare. Perhaps at work when things have overwhelmed you, nip to the rest room and just send those roots down for a minute or two.

Grounding crystals

There are also crystals that can be used to help you ground, hold them in your hand or keep them in your pocket, some suggestions to use are:

Amethyst, calcite (orange), carnelian, fluorite, hematite, jasper, kyanite, labradorite, obsidian (black), petrified wood, pyrite, quartz (rose), quartz (smoky), tiger's eye or tourmaline.

But a good 'ole natural pebble will also do the trick.

Check out the other earth crystals in this book, they may work well for you.

Grounding herbs

You could make yourself a grounding medicine pouch and fill it with herbs that help to keep your energy stable such as:

Beech, cornflower (batchelor's buttons), cramp bark, cypress, dogwood, echinacea, grass, honesty, honeysuckle, horsetail, knotweed, lungwort, magnolia, mugwort, patchouli, plantain, primrose, sorrel, tulip, valerian, vervain, yew. Check out the list of earth related herbs in this book, they may work for you.

Grounding food

Eating is an excellent way to calm your energy, chocolate is my go-to food after energy work and the aforementioned cake works well too. I also find the following foods particularly good for grounding: Barley, beetroot, borage, bread, cake, cookies, pistachio, potato, rice.

Exercise: Try out different types of grounding exercises, crystals, herbs and food and see which ones work best. Keep a record of which ones you worked with and how effective they were.

Centring

Centring is finding that inner calm within ourselves, which allows us to regroup and focus. Our centre is where our magic comes from and where the divine in us resides.

The centre isn't in the same place for everyone, for some it will be somewhere in the stomach area (solar plexus) for others it will be in the chest at the heart centre. Or it could be somewhere else entirely. You can find yours by visualising two beams of white light, one coming into the crown of your head, the other coming up from the ground. The two beams will meet somewhere within your body, where they do, that is your centre.

Centring Exercise: After you have done the grounding exercise is a good time to centre yourself:

See a beam of bright light enter from the sky into the top of your head (crown chakra).

See a second beam of light from the earth enter from the base or your spine (root chakra).

See the two beams meet at your centre where they swirl together and form a ball of energy.

Go inside and connect with this power source within. Feel it and see it glowing and pulsating. This is where your magic comes from.

Feel a sense of calm that comes from this connection with your centre and the divine spark within.

When you are ready, see the beams of light slowly withdraw and the ball of energy start to fade. You may want to leave it as a small light glowing within.

When you are ready, return to the here and now.

Ideally grounding and centring should become part of your daily practice but after any magical work.

The Elementals

The Elementals are the energies of nature itself; they are the forces of the elements. They are true energy and have the characteristics of the element they belong to. They can take on any shape, size or form to deal with a particular task.

Elementals can charge us with energy; they can work with us on a physical, mental, emotional and spiritual level. Learning to work with them can tune us in to connect with the energy of nature around us. The Elementals interweave their energy patterns to create and keep all of nature, all of life on our planet.

Elementals have nothing to obstruct them, they can move through matter with ease, but they also need to connect with us to help with their own spiritual growth and evolution.

In ancient Greece they were referred to as the kings of the four winds. Ancient Egyptians saw them as four sons of Horus. And the Norse had four dwarves, each one holding up a corner of the world.

In modern Wicca each group of Elementals has a higher being that looks over them, a King. Overseeing the Kings are Archangels. It is quite a hierarchical set up.

There are, as you know four elements, so there are four

Elementals, four Elemental Kings and four Archangels. The Earth elementals are known as gnomes, their King is Ghob and the Archangel is Uriel/Auriel. The elementals in their lower forms (i.e. gnomes), the rulers or the Archangels can be called in as quarters when in ritual, as well as called upon to lend their energy to spell work or to meet in meditation.

Archangel Uriel/Auriel

Uriel is the Archangel of wisdom, inspiration and motivation. Interestingly his name translates as 'Fire or Light', which doesn't really connect with Earth, but who am I to argue?

He is an angel of magical power and force. He also covers all things astrological and alchemy. Uriel is the holder of the keys to hell. This dude is one of the most powerful archangels.

I will be completely honest here; I don't work with angels or Archangels at all. But if you are drawn to do so, follow your intuition. However, if you are put off by the thought of angels being Christian, remember that the idea of angels is found in many cultures and they predate Christianity. Basically, angels are universal.

King Ghob

King Ghob (or Gob) is the ruler of the elemental gnomes and is said to rule with a magic sword and to be an influence over the 'melancholic temperament of man'. He lives in the woodlands and the forests, but also within the caves and underground. Together with Uriel they control the land and the plants of this world. He is said to be shy and his looks are of one slightly beaten by life, perhaps after dealing with mankind? But his power is unquestionable, as is his strength.

Gnomes

The Gnome is the archetypal spirit of Earth. Try not to think of the gnome you know from fairy tale stories, the Elemental Gnome is very earthy, but their form and shape can vary immensely, and they can change to suit their situation.

Earth Elementals maintain our planet, the structure itself. They create the forests, the trees, the plants and the flowers. They design all the crystals and rocks; they are very skilled craftsmen. They work very closely with nature. They are the beings that put the energy into all the rocks, pebbles and crystals.

An Earth Elemental can help us to attune to nature; they can work with us to help maintain our own physical bodies. They can help us develop all our senses, to look after ourselves, to feel grounded and connected. Working with them can give us determination, appreciation, openness and spontaneity.

Be careful though, too much work with just the Earth Elemental and you might find yourself feeling cynical, sceptical and overly cautious.

Earth Elemental shapeshifting meditation: Close your eyes and take a few deep breaths. Feel yourself becoming calm and relaxed with each out breath, letting go of all the worries of the day. Feel any tension leave your body as we prepare to shape shift with the element of Earth.

Turn to face North the direction of the element of earth. Visualise, feel and sense the element in whatever form is appropriate for you. This could be a mountain, a silent cave, a majestic tree, or your favourite spot in your garden, focus on that image.

Breathe it in, deep down into your abdomen and into your being. Let the element of earth spread throughout your entire body until you feel yourself dissolve and you become earth.

Stay with this element for a couple of breaths... gradually let the earth recede from your body until it is only in your belly then release it completely with your next out breath.

Take a few deeper breaths now and when you are ready open your eyes. Welcome back to your human form.

Exercise: Work with the elemental meditation and keep a record of your experiences.

Ancestors and Spirits of the Land

Every single piece of land, wherever your feet land, will have an energy. It may also have echoes of your ancestors, those that have lived there before. Even in big cities you will find energy beneath your feet and in the buildings. Before the office blocks and houses were built, there would have been a whole history of structures or people work and living on the land before.

I believe it pays to connect with the ancestors or energies of the land where you live. It can really help your magic to tap into that ancient vibe. I have a real connection with the area that I live in and it helps me to feel grounded and give me a sense of belonging. Whenever I am out and about, particularly when hosting a ritual for instance, I will connect with the energy, the ancestors and the spirits of the land. It is only good manners after all, if you are going to be holding a ritual or event on their land it will behove you to ask permission from the spirits first.

One word of warning; please do be careful when sending out your spidery senses to connect. Some places have a very terrible history and it can be quite upsetting to tap into that. Just be wary and perhaps don't open up when on the site of a huge and bloody battle!

There are certain places and locations that align with the element or earth. If you can take yourself off to visit them to connect. If that isn't possible crack out your visualisation skills and meditate to take yourself there.

Exercise: Take a look at the earth places mentioned here. Do some research in your local area and see how many of these types of places you can find or even visit. Keep notes on your experiences.

Caves

There is something very primordial about caves. They hold a

certain mystery within the darkness. They also make me think of the Crone goddess. Most caves are carved or hollowed into rock which gives them a large earth element energy.

Cave meditation: Find a quiet place where you won't be disturbed and make yourself comfortable. Take a few deep breaths in and out.

As your world around you dissipates you find yourself standing on a seashore, cool sand beneath your feet, blue sky above you and a fresh breeze dancing around you.

Take your shoes off and wriggle your toes in the sand.

Breath in the fresh air and take in your surroundings. As you turn you see a large opening in the rock face behind you. Realising it is a cave you are drawn towards it. Walking through the sand with your bare feet you reach the cave entrance.

The air is cooler inside and the sand feels cold but pleasant underfoot.

Just inside the entrance you see a large pile of pebbles. Beside them it looks as if someone has started to lay them out in a spiral. You pick up a pebble and add it to the spiral, then you add another, and another. Slowly and surely you add pebbles to create a larger spiral shape.

When you add the last pebble, you realise the spiral fills the entire floor of the cave.

You start to walk the spiral as it sweeps in loops around the cave.

Ever decreasing, allow your thoughts to flow as you walk the spiral.

Taking you on a journey inward. In the dark protective, safe sanctum of the cave the spiral takes you on an inward journey.

When you reach the centre of the spiral you sit down.

Surrounded by the walls of rock to your sides and above you, pebbles all around and sand beneath your feet. You are in a womb of the earth element.

Spend some time here.

Look inwards for messages, images and insights.

When you are ready, stand up and slowly walk the spiral again. This time following as it flows outwards. The curve of the spiral takes you back to the cave opening.

Glance back at the spiral and into the darkness of the cave.

Know that it is here, should you wish to return.

Take a step out from the cave and into the light.

Wriggle your toes in the sand and gently come back to this reality. Open your eyes and wriggle your fingers and toes.

Canyons

A canyon is defined as a deep, often narrow gorge, ravine or valley in the landscape, often with a river flowing through the bottom. It is surrounded by high cliffs and can be very deep. They are usually created over a very long period of time by erosion from running water.

Canyon meditation: Find a quiet place where you won't be disturbed and make yourself comfortable. Take a few deep breaths in and out.

As your world around you dissipates you find yourself standing on the top of a cliff. Stretching out in front of you is a large canyon. The sun is shining and bouncing light on the sides of the rock slopes. Beautiful reds, oranges and yellows, the sides of the canyon seem to sparkle.

Something glints at the very bottom of the canyon and you can just make out a river meandering along through the base.

A noise startles you and turning around you see a dog not far from where you stand.

It looks up and barks at you, whilst wagging its tail.

You put out your hand and the dog steps forward, giving your hand a sniff, then bends its head for you to scratch its ears.

The dog then turns and walks away, stopping and looking back. It seems he wants you to follow.

As you step forward the dog starts walking and you go with him.

The dog leads you to a pathway carved into the sides of the canyon, leading downwards.

It is steep, but safe under foot.

You reach a flat level on the pathway and the dog stops. He nudges a loose pebble towards you with his nose.

You pick up the pebble and feel the need to send any negative energy, feelings or vibes into the small stone. Then you pull back your arm and throw the pebble, up into the air and watch as it drops downwards. Further and further into the canyon below. So far that you lose sight of it.

The dog nudges another pebble over and you release more negative energy, frustration and emotions flowing into the stone and then throw, watching it as it drops down into the depths of the canyon.

Now take a moment to ground yourself and think about all the positives you have in your life.

Feeling much better and more light-hearted you gaze around you, taking in the vastness of the canyon. How tall the rocks are rising above you and how deep the canyon falls down below. A huge chasm in the surface of Mother Nature.

A warm nose nuzzles your hand and you turn to see the dog, ready to lead you back down the pathway.

With each step back down, you feel lighter and happier until you arrive back where you began.

Now slowly and gently come back to this reality. Open your eyes and wriggle your fingers and toes.

Forests

A forest is large with the trees packed in so tightly that barely any sunlight makes its way through the canopy of leaves. Forests can have deciduous or evergreen trees or a mixture of both, but they cover a large area and are full of lots of different wildlife. They will also have shrubs, undergrowth and grasses. Did you know that there are also different types of forest? This depends on the location in the world. Boreal forests are found near the poles, tropical forests around the equator and the mid latitude area has temperate forests.

Forest meditation: Find a quiet place where you won't be disturbed and make yourself comfortable. Take a few deep breaths in and out.

As your world around you dissipates you find yourself in the centre of a dark forest. The canopy overhead is dense with green leaves. Around you are thick tree trunks as far as you can see. The ground beneath your feet is thick with layers of fallen leaves, pinecones, moss and ferns.

You breathe in deeply; the sweet earthy scent fills your nose.

Listen carefully and you will hear the rustle of leaves in the breeze, the birds high above you and the wildlife in the undergrowth.

There is a small space around you, almost a clearing.

Lay down on the ground, it is surprisingly comfortable lying on the carpet of leaves. Reach out and feel the leaves and forest floor with your hands.

The scent of the earth fills your noise and you breathe in deeply.

Lay quietly and look above you at the canopy of leaves.

What symbols or messages do you see that the leaves and branches make against the small glimpses of sky?

Now listen, what do you hear?

There is a snuffling sound as an animal makes its way through the ferns and leaves.

*A small badger comes into view, it is rummaging around in the
forest floor and comes right up to your feet.*

It sniffs then turns and wanders back into the forest.

Lay here for as long as you need to.

*When you are ready sit gently up. Noticing something by your
foot you realise the badger must have left a gift for you. What is it?*

Pick it up and put it in your pocket.

Stand now and take a long look around.

Know that you can come back here at any time.

Now slowly and gently come back to this reality. Open your eyes
and wriggle your fingers and toes.

Groves

A grove is a small group of trees with minimal or no undergrowth
which can be made up from any type of tree but often fruit trees.

Grove meditation: Find a quiet place where you won't be disturbed
and make yourself comfortable. Take a few deep breaths in and
out.

*As your world around you dissipates you find yourself standing
in a grassy clearing, the sky is blue but there is a crisp autumn feel
to the air.*

*Looking around you realise you are standing in a circle of trees,
a grove of nut trees.*

Walk slowly around the circle of trees.

*Notice the leaves and fallen nuts on the ground. Pick up any
that you are drawn to. Feel the texture of the autumn leaves and
the shell casing of the nuts. What sort of nut is it? What shape are
the leaves?*

*Stand in the centre of the grove and turn slowly around, looking
carefully at each tree. Send out a request to connect with one of
them.*

When you get a response, walk up to that tree and put both hands on the trunk. You feel an immediate connection. Ask the tree any questions you might have and listen to the answers...

When you are ready thank the tree.

Take one last wander around the grove of trees and when you are ready, slowly and gently come back to this reality.

Open your eyes and wriggle your fingers and toes.

Valleys

The definition of a valley is a low area of land that lies between mountains or hills. It often has a stream or a river running through the bottom.

Valley meditation: Find a quiet place where you won't be disturbed and make yourself comfortable. Take a few deep breaths in and out.

As your world around you dissipates you find yourself standing on a grassy riverbank. Take a look around at the scenery.

The lush green grass beneath your feet is sprinkled with white daisy flowers and bright yellow buttercups.

The sky above you is bright blue and the sun is shining.

Up on either side of you, grass covered hills rise above.

Listening you can hear the bubbling and trickling of the water as it bounces along the riverbed beside you.

Then you hear the tinkling sound of bells. And look around you for the source.

Coming down the hillside is a large goat wearing a bell around its neck. He has large majestic horns that curl back from his head and a long shaggy coat of fur. He is followed by several smaller goats and two small baby kid goats.

They carefully make their way down the slope until they reach the river's edge.

Lowering his head, the billy goat takes a drink from the water. The other goats follow his lead.

With the two kid goats paddling and splashing in the shallow water at the edge beside them.

You watch them drink and the small ones play, so full of fun and mischief.

Take a moment to think about what energy or messages goat can help you with or how it reflects on any situation in your own life.

Goat brings strength, independence, survival, security and foundation. He also provides direction and new pathways.

When they have finished with the river, the goats turn and head off in a new direction. Following the river as it winds its way through the valley.

You watch as they disappear into the distance.

Then you notice something on the riverbank where the goats have been. Walk over and pick it up, it is a bell that must have fallen from one of their collars.

What does this symbolise for you?

Hold the bell in your hands and spend some time contemplating.

When you are ready take a last look around you taking in the scenery. Know that you can come back to this place any time.

Allow yourself to slowly come back to this reality. Open your eyes and wriggle your fingers and toes.

Fields and Meadows

Field, meadow, pasture and fen...lots of different names but what do they mean?

A meadow is generally a small agricultural grassland sometimes spattered with wildflowers that is not intensively managed. They are often poor soil and not easily accessible by farm machinery. A meadow usually has a boundary made from old stone walls, woodland or hedges.

A field however is very similar to a meadow but will be

managed more intensively usually filled with a particular crop. A field comes in all shapes and sizes, freshly ploughed soil, new shoots of crops or full with grown grains or vegetables.

Field meditation: Find a quiet place where you won't be disturbed and make yourself comfortable. Take a few deep breaths in and out.

As your world around you dissipates you find yourself standing on the edge of a field. Stretching out in front of you is a newly ploughed field, the rich brown soil neatly laying in furrows.

The sky above you is clear and the air is fresh but not cold.

The field is surrounded by a wild looking hedgerow and you watch as birds fly in and out.

Movement catches your attention as a rabbit hops out from beneath one of the hedges.

He looks up and around and takes a few hops further into the field. As he moves out, another rabbit follows him, emerging from beneath the foliage of the hedgerow.

As you watch, several more rabbits make their way into the field, crossing the fresh brown soil.

Your eye is drawn to what seems to be a man standing in the centre of the field. You walk across to meet him.

The closer you get you realise it isn't a person but a scarecrow. Dressed in a large floppy hat and dusty overcoat he has a scarf wrapped around his neck and gloves tied to the poles where his hands would be. His head is a piece of sack with a face crudely painted on.

A gust of wind whips past and takes his hat right off his head. It lands by your feet, so you bend and pick it up.

As your hand touches the hat your head is filled with images. You have tapped into the energy of the hat, the scarecrow and the history they hold. What do you see, what do you hear or feel? What does it mean to you?

Take some time to process your thoughts.
Then place the hat back on the scarecrows head.
You jump as you are sure you heard a faint "thank you" ...
Turn and make your way back across the field to the hedgerow.
Take a last look around.

Slowly and gently come back to this reality. Open your eyes and wriggle your fingers and toes.

Farms

There are all types of farms; arable, dairy, livestock, produce or a combination. They all have their own unique energy. Please don't wander on to a farm without permission. Not only is it impolite (and trespassing) but farmyards can be dangerous places. You might find a farm in your area that has a farm shop which is a great place to buy produce.

Farm meditation: Find a quiet place where you won't be disturbed and make yourself comfortable. Take a few deep breaths in and out.

As your world around you dissipates you find yourself standing in a farmyard. Beneath your feet is mud and there is a smell in the air of hay and animals.

It is very early in the morning and the sky is still dark, with the sun rise just beginning.

There are large barns on either side of you and a brick farmhouse at the end of the yard in front of you.

A gate opens behind you with a loud metallic click.

You hear the sounds of cows mooing loudly and the clip clop of their hooves as they leave the grass of the field and enter the hard courtyard.

You step back as they move past you, seemingly knowing exactly which way they are heading.

They bring a warm wave of air with them.

As the last one comes through the gate you follow them into the barn they have now filled.

Heading through the large barn doors you are hit with the sound of milking machines and cows mooing contentedly and munching as they eat big bales of hay that are strung up for them.

The noise is loud but somehow comforting.

You find a pile of hay bales and sit, watching and listening to all that is happening around you.

This is earth magic in action; fertility, productivity, stability and the magical energy of contentment surrounds you.

Draw upon that energy, where do you need it in your own life?

Movement disturbs you from your thoughts as the herd is now moving back out of the barn.

You follow them, out through the doors, across the farmyard and to the large metal gate.

Watch them as they re-enter a large grassy field. They look happy and relaxed.

Take a last look around and then slowly come back to this reality.

Open your eyes and wriggle your fingers and toes.

Gardens

It doesn't matter if your garden is a tiny concrete patio or acres of manicured lawn (or all the variations in between). Gardens are beautiful places to be. Sit in your own garden or seek out a local pubic one.

Garden meditation: Find a quiet place where you won't be disturbed and make yourself comfortable. Take a few deep breaths in and out.

As your world around you dissipates you find yourself standing outside a large stately home. It is an enormous grand building, beautifully majestic.

The air is cold, but you are dressed to keep warm. Under foot is a light dusting of snow that crunches as you walk.

Laid out in front of the house is one of the most breath-taking gardens you have ever seen.

All of the garden is smothered in a blanket of pure white snow. Like a patchwork quilt laid out in front of you, there are pathways, clipped hedges and bare trees.

You are drawn to enter the pathway that leads through the middle of the garden.

Making fresh footprints in the virgin snow, you investigate.

There are paths leading off at angles, hedges, bushes and bare branch trees, skeletons of summer plants and seed heads covered in frost. Sparkling like jewels in a winter wonderland.

As you wander, a flash of red streaks across in front of you.

Quickly you follow, but quietly. You arrive at the centre of the garden and a large water fountain that has frozen, with icicles dripping from the top.

Sitting quite confidently in front of the fountain, is a fox. His red orange coat a bright contrast to the white snow.

He looks at you, really right at you, there is a connection.

Fox brings cunning, courage, persistence, patience and compassion.

Does he have a message for you? Or perhaps the answer to a question you might have?

Spend some time with him.

Then quick as a flash, he is gone.

Trace your steps now, back out of the garden to the place you began.

Slowly and gently come back to this reality. Open your eyes and wriggle your fingers and toes.

Parks

A park is defined as a public garden or land used for recreation. It might be your local park or something grander but even the largest city has a park or two.

Park meditation: Find a quiet place where you won't be disturbed and make yourself comfortable. Take a few deep breaths in and out.

As your world around you dissipates you find yourself standing in the centre of a children's playground. It is dusk and the park is empty, you are alone.

Now is the time to let out your inner child.

What does the playground have? Swings? A slide? Roundabout? Bouncy things or climbing frames?

Explore, really explore. Try everything. You are never too old and never too big.

Have fun and experience it all as if you were five years old.

When you are completely exhausted and have been on everything, sit yourself down on a park bench to reflect.

You need more of this in your life...

And when you are ready, slowly and gently come back to this reality.

Open your eyes and wriggle your fingers and toes.

Kitchens

I love my kitchen; it is a place where I feel very at home. In an ideal world it would be huge and have a large kitchen table in the middle for all the family to sit around. In reality I live in a terraced town house with a small, but practical kitchen. Sometimes we must work with what we have!

Kitchen meditation: Find a quiet place where you won't be disturbed and make yourself comfortable. Take a few deep breaths in and out.

As your world around you dissipates you find yourself standing in a doorway inside a large castle. The walls around you are stone and the floor beneath you is made from huge stone slabs.

Step through the doorway and into the kitchen...

With a great high ceiling, the kitchen stretches on forever and is full of people bustling around preparing food.

To one side is a massive fireplace filled with a cast iron range, covered in bubbling pots and pans.

Wooden tables stretch down the centre where people are making pastries, breads and cakes. Others are preparing huge mounds of vegetables and fruits.

At one end of the table there is a space, with what looks to be a mound of bread dough. Looking around there doesn't seem to be anyone tending to it. So, you take on the job.

The dough is soft but sticky, so you dust the table with flour and start to knead. Backwards and forwards with your hands, manipulating the dough as it becomes softer and lighter.

You pop the now well kneaded dough into a bowl and put a cloth over the top. Leaving it to prove.

Someone hands you a large mug full of steaming hot liquid that smells of cinnamon and ginger. Finding a spare seat and sitting, you sip your drink and watch the business going on around you.

Feeling calm and grounded you reflect on how busy your life is and what changes could be made...

When you have finished your drink, you pop the mug on the table and quietly slip back out of the kitchen.

And when you are ready, slowly and gently come back to this reality.

Open your eyes and wriggle your fingers and toes.

Mines

Whenever I think of mines my thoughts go straight to the fairy tale of Snow White. The dwarves all underground digging for precious gems. Of course, there are mines for jewels, but we also have mines for all kinds of metals and minerals including salt, gold, silver, iron ore, copper and tin.

Mines meditation: Find a quiet place where you won't be disturbed and make yourself comfortable. Take a few deep breaths in and out.

As your world around you dissipates you find yourself standing at the base of a cliff, beside you is an archway cut into the hillside.

The entrance is lit with lamps that seem to go right the way back in.

Enter the archway...

The walls of the tunnel are pure white and when you reach out and touch them, they feel slightly warm.

The light from the lamps makes the white walls glisten and sparkle.

As you make your way further down you reach the top of a wooden staircase leading down.

Holding onto the handrail you slowly make your way down.

The lamps continue along your pathway, shining light onto the white sparkling walls, ceiling and floors.

When you reach the bottom of the stairway you find yourself in a large cavern. It is enormous. Huge white walls stretching up as far as you can see to a white ceiling way up above you. All around you is white.

In the centre there appears to be a wooden seat, so you make your way over.

As you sit down you notice a small water fountain behind the bench. Lean over and put your hands in the water.

It is cold, icy cold.

You lift your fingers to your lips and taste the water.

Salt! The water is very salty.

Now that you look around, you realise you are inside a salt mine. Everything around you is pure solid salt; the floor beneath your feet, the walls around you and the ceiling above you, all solid salt.

You can still taste the salt on your lips, sit quietly now and reflect on the qualities of salt and what it means to you…

When you are ready stand up and make your way back over to the foot of the stairs.

Place your hands on the wall of the salt mine, draw in energy, take as much as you need.

Then slowly and carefully make your way back up the staircase. Walk back along the entrance way and out into the sunlight.

And when you are ready, slowly and gently come back to this reality. Open your eyes and wriggle your fingers and toes.

Holes and Chasms

A hole could be a tiny thing or something much larger, it can also be physical (a hole in your jumper) or emotional (a hole left in your life). Essentially a hole is a hollow place in a surface. A chasm however is a whole (no pun intended) other thing. A chasm is a deep fissure in the surface of the earth. Whether it is a tiny mouse hole or a huge meteor crash site, holes can be interesting places to explore…

Hole meditation: Find a quiet place where you won't be disturbed and make yourself comfortable. Take a few deep breaths in and out.

As your world around you dissipates you find yourself in a field standing beside a grassy bank. The sky above you is dark and the moon and stars are shining down upon you.

Looking at the bank of grass and earth you notice a small brown package tied with string just by your feet.

Pick it up and unwrap it...

Inside the parcel is a cookie, take a bite...

A strange feeling comes over you and you realise you are shrinking; your whole body is slowly getting smaller and smaller. Until you end up the size of a mouse.

Everything around you looks huge, even the blades of grass are enormous.

Then you spot a small hole in the earth just at the base of a clump of grass.

Carefully you climb into the hole.

The soil is dry and the air inside the hole is warm and musty. Slowly and carefully you make your way further into the hole.

You feel comfortable and safe as you explore further...

Above you roots of plants dangle down from the roof of the hole and the walls are studded with pebbles and stones. Reach out and touch them, feel the earth energy within.

Then you hear a snuffling noise, very faint but rustling towards you.

Stop to listen more carefully.

Then a snout appears in the darkness, a nose sniffs you...

It is the owner of the burrow you are in, a very friendly, but shy mole. Wearing his dark velvety fur with a pink snuffly nose.

He stops right in front of you and you feel the need to talk to him. Do so, ask him any questions that you want. He may have great insight for you...

When you are finished, thank the mole for his guidance.

Turn and carefully make your way back through the tunnel to the entrance.

Stop just as you see the daylight and spend a few moments with your hands placed against the warm soil walls.

Breathe in and fill your body with the energy from the earth.

When you are ready step to the entrance. There you find another small package, brown paper wrapped with string.

Untie it and inside you find another cookie, take a bite.

Slowly you feel yourself growing larger, eventually back to your usual size, you are now standing once again outside the grassy bank.

Take a last look around, remember what was said to you and gently come back to this reality.

Open your eyes and wriggle your fingers and toes.

Libraries

One of the most fascinating indoor places ever. Libraries hold so much adventure, mystery, intrigue, wisdom and reference. Each book waiting patiently for you to open the cover and jump right in. There is also something peaceful about stepping into a library too.

Library meditation: Find a quiet place where you won't be disturbed and make yourself comfortable. Take a few deep breaths in and out.

As your world around you dissipates you find yourself standing in front of a large wooden door set into the pale stone of a grand building.

Reach out and open the door, it creaks as it swings inwards.

Step inside...

What you find are shelves of books, going back as far as the eye can see and stretching right up to the very ceiling. Wall upon wall of books. Shelf upon shelf filled with tomes of interest. Books are also piled up in stacks all over the floor.

Breathe in deeply, take in the air.

Listen carefully, to the silence.

Take a walk around and investigate...

Pick up any books that you are drawn to look at, feel the earth energy from the covers and pages.

Behind one of the shelves is a book stand, with one book set carefully on top, the pages open.

Take a look...

This is the book you need to see; these are the pages you need to read; this is the information the library wants you to find...

Take some time to read the open pages and think about what it means to you.

When you are ready continue to look around if you feel drawn to...

Then make your way back to the door at the entrance.

Know that you can come back here any time you are seeking insight or advice.

And when you are ready, slowly and gently come back to this reality. Open your eyes and wriggle your fingers and toes.

Garden centres and Greenhouses

One of my favourite places to visit. A garden centre or nursery is filled with nature that you can take home and transplant into your own space. And of course, it also supplies the tools and materials to create your garden too, such as fertiliser and compost. A lot of garden centres are created inside large glasshouses/greenhouses, so they have a very particular feel to them. Some of you may even have your own greenhouse at home. I am very lucky to own a small greenhouse (we call her Gertie), it is definitely a very earthy place to be, as well as productive.

Glasshouse meditation: Find a quiet place where you won't be disturbed and make yourself comfortable. Take a few deep breaths in and out.

As your world around you dissipates you find yourself inside an enormous glass house. The air is warm and damp, but you feel comfortable.

The glass ceiling rises way above you and the light is streaming in on all sides through the glass panes. There is dark soil beneath your feet and all around you are large plants and greenery.

The pathway you are standing on leads around the glasshouse, so you begin to follow it.

Take a look on either side of you as you walk and don't forget to look above you too.

What plants do you see? Look at the variety of colours, shapes and sizes.

Reach out and touch the leaves, the flowers and the fruits. Feel the different textures.

Can you see any insects on the plants?

As you round a bend in the path you come to a large potting bench filled with lush, rich dark brown soil. Beside it, a stack of terracotta plant pots on one side and a tray of seedlings on the other.

Come up to the bench and start filling the pots with soil, feel the texture of the earth in your hands.

Then begin to transplant each seedling, firming it carefully into each pot of soil.

Repeat with the pots until the seedlings are all in their new homes.

Look and find a watering can, use it to shower the plants with fresh water.

Stand back and take a look at what you have created, the beginnings of new growth. How does this reflect your own life? What meaning can you take from it?

When you are ready continue following the path and making new plant discoveries.

Make a mental note of any that particularly stand out to you. They may have meaning.

Once back at the beginning of the pathway again, remember what you have seen and reflect on any insights you have gained.

And when you are ready, slowly and gently come back to this reality. Open your eyes and wriggle your fingers and toes.

Farmers Markets

Farmers markets and farm shops are brilliant places to purchase locally grown produce. Usually organic and always in season, which makes the product taste so much better. Look around for one in your area. They often sell everything from fruit and vegetables to meat, chutney and honey.

Farmers market meditation: Find a quiet place where you won't be disturbed and make yourself comfortable. Take a few deep breaths in and out.

As your world around you dissipates you find yourself standing on a cobbled street at the start of a busy market.

There are stalls stretching out in front of you on either side of the street.

Different coloured canopies, all filled with interesting produce.

The air is full of noise, people chatting and stall holders calling out.

Start to walk up one side of the street, taking in each stall and the produce that it has on offer.

Pick up anything that you feel the need to touch, smell the scent and take in all the details.

Some stalls have taster pots with their wares set out for you try, savour the tastes.

What produce particularly takes your attention?

As you reach the far end of the street there is one stall that doesn't appear to have any produce. But you are drawn to walk up and speak to the vendor. They greet you politely and you ask what they are selling.

Listen to the reply...

This stall has whatever you really need, perhaps not what you want, but definitely what you need...

The vendor talks to you, listen carefully. Once your conversation is finished, they hand you an item to take away with you. What were you given and what does it mean to you? Ask the vendor more questions if you need to.

When you are ready, turn and walk back down the other side of the street, looking at the stalls as you pass each one. Investigate closer if you feel drawn to.

Once back at the beginning take another look at the item you were given. Think back on anything that was said to you.

And when you are ready, slowly and gently come back to this reality. Open your eyes and wriggle your fingers and toes.

Basements and Cellars

Whenever I think of a basement it conjures up images of horror films or murders...on TV whenever anyone goes down into the basement, they very rarely come back up. In reality the basement is usually full of junk and/or washing machines. Not usually creatures from the deep or axe wielding murderers. They are in fact a very good place to visualise when working with your shadow self, areas in your subconscious that can be investigated. Usually memories or personality traits that you don't really want to delve in to, but sometimes it can really help to clear out those vibes.

Basement meditation: Find a quiet place where you won't be disturbed and make yourself comfortable. Take a few deep breaths in and out.

As your world around you dissipates you find yourself standing at the top of a rough wooden staircase. It leads down into darkness.

You feel safe and comfortable and very much drawn to investigate what lies at the bottom of the stairs, so you head downwards.

At the bottom of the staircase your hand stumbles upon a switch, press it. And as you do so, a light flickers into being and the room is illuminated with a soft warm glow.

Look around the basement room.

There are boxes stacked around the edges, all different sizes and shapes.

Each one has a word written on the side.

Have a look at each of the words, which one are you drawn to open?

When you find the one you want to look at, take the box down and set it in the centre of the room.

Open the lid and see what is inside...

Take out any items that you find, what do they mean to you?

Spend some time looking through the box and thinking carefully about the meaning behind it.

Once you are done with the first box, take a look around and see if there is another that you feel drawn to investigate. If there is, take it down and look inside.

Spend as much time as you need...

When you are ready, put the boxes back neatly where you found them.

Make your way to the bottom of the stairs and flick the light switch off.

Head back up the staircase.

And when you are ready, slowly and gently come back to this reality. Open your eyes and wriggle your fingers and toes.

Crossroads

Any crossroads is a very magical place, whether it is the centre of a dirt pathway in the woods, country lanes meeting or even a main road. That point at the middle where the roads all cross is very special. It is the meeting place of all the four directions and therefore all four elements. (Although some crossroads are created by three and not four pathways). The centre of a crossroads links the two worlds, the living and the dead. It is an 'in between' place. Many traditions have deities that are associated with crossroads too, such as Elegba, Rah and Hecate. Hoodoo tricks and spells are also buried at the crossroads to work their magic. Candle stubs and remains of worked spells can also be buried here. Even a bridge crossing over a stream can also create a crossroad. Definitely a magical spot and one where transformation happens. It has power, potential and offers up all sorts of choices and decisions.

Crossroads meditation: Find somewhere quiet where you won't be disturbed. Close your eyes and focus on your breathing, deep breaths in, deep breaths out.

As your world around you dissipates you find yourself standing at the centre of a crossroads. It is sunrise and the sky is a beautiful colour.

Turn and look around you. There are four pathways, each one leading off in a different direction.

You have a question to ask.

Turn slowly to face each direction, one at a time. As you face each pathway ask your question. Wait to see if you can hear an answer.

Once you have asked your question to each direction think about which one answered you. Did any of them give a response? Do you feel drawn to walk down any particular one?

Make your choice.

Take the pathway that you were drawn to.

Start walking.

Take note of the foliage, if any that you see at the side of the pathway. Reach out and touch the plants that you see.

Keep an eye out for any animals you might see along the way.

You may even meet a person as you walk.

Then you reach your destination.

Where has the pathway led you?

What or who is at the end?

Ask more questions, seek answers from whatever or whomever is there.

This is the decision you made, and this is the direction that might be most beneficial for you to take. Give it some serious thought. Why where you led here?

What relevance does it have to your real life?

If you feel drawn to, walk back along the pathway to the centre and ask another question. You may be led down a second pathway.

If not, stand in the centre and take a last look around.

Then slowly and gently come back to this reality. Open your eyes and wriggle your fingers and toes.

Pathways and Ley Lines

Every road and pathway lead from somewhere, to somewhere. I like to work with them for new beginnings and finding the right direction. Walking meditations work well, doesn't matter if you are walking on the beach, in a woodland or on the pavement. Each step can take you deeper into meditation. This is particularly useful if you are looking for answers to a decision or to find a new direction or way out of a situation. Please do be careful, don't walk along a main road pavement beside a busy road whilst meditating!

Ley lines are called many different names, dragon lines or spirit lines in some cases. They are all different names for the same thing. These are lines of energy, straight and often geometric, that run across the land. Generally found to connect ancient sacred sites or natural features. Standing stones, henges and hill forts for instance. You cannot see the lines, but they are there, energy pathways that criss-cross all over the globe.

There are also ancient pathways or trackways. Often referred to as 'otherworldly paths' that were once followed for religious processions or celebrations. These will also have a special energy.

You can connect to the earth wherever you are, but I do think that certain landscapes lend themselves more to magic. Perhaps the more history the land holds, the more energy there is to tap in to? Some places are even thought to be bad luck or have the reputation of being a 'contrary place'. These places hold myths and legends of being a fairy travelled track. Often pathways where the dead were carried to church hold the idea of being bad luck too.

There is also the suggestion that ley lines are connected to astronomical points as well, some of the lines lining up to the path of the sun on certain festival dates for instance. Geometry has also been thrown into the mix with the idea that megalithic building crews not only worked with astronomy but also geometry when placing their structures.

I think personally it has to be how you feel about a place, have a look at local maps and seek out the ley lines and also take note of old folk names for places because a lot of them will have been derived from the Faery or events that happened in the past and these will carry strong energies.

Exercise: Find out where the ley lines are in your area and visit some of the spots especially where they cross. Record what energy you felt.

Burial Sites and Standing Stones

Some areas will have a whole host of ancient and sacred sites that are quite obvious. Other places may take some investigating to find. Check your local library and the internet for burial mounds, standing stones and ancient sites. These places are fascinating and will hold a really interesting amount of energy to explore.

Exercise: Find out if there are any sacred or ancient sites in your area and visit some of them. Record what energy you felt.

Earth Matters

Soil and Earth

Soil and earth, well dirt basically, and it comes in many forms. Some soil is light and sandy and others (like the stuff in my garden) is thick and clay like and any manner of types in between, but essentially it is full of magic. Soil is obviously aligned with the element of earth, but it holds a definite life force as it is jammed pack full of nutrients to feed the plants. Earth is grounding and solid, bringing stability and strength with it. It doesn't matter if you are standing knee deep in mud at a festival or on concrete paving in a shopping centre, the earth is there beneath your feet. Soil, earth, dirt, mud, graveyard dirt and clay are all different forms with the same source.

Soil can be used in all sorts of magical workings and as always go with your intuition, but I tend to use it for the following:

Soil magical properties:
Fertility, nurturing, stabilising, grounding, manifestation, prosperity, employment, home, protection, rebirth.
Uses: Burying, planting, making mandalas and drawing sigils with and in. Also use in magic pouches, sachet powder and witch bottles.

It's a Salty Situation

Salt is one of the most used items to represent the element of earth. Salt being a very powerful, magical ingredient is also often seen on a witch's altar to represent the element of earth. Salt used to be a very valuable commodity which was once used as currency. It was also a vital preserving agent to conserve food and prevent starvation through the winter months.

You don't need to spend lots of money and buy fancy schmancy salt that was collected by flying nuns from a hidden

Tibetan monastery on a Friday at noon whilst hopping on one leg and chanting prayers...no matter what poncey name it has and whether it is black, white, pink or grey...use whatever you have in your kitchen cupboard...SALT IS SALT...

Salt is a crystalline mineral made of two elements, sodium (Na) and chlorine (Cl). Most of the world's salt is harvested from salt mines or by evaporating sea water or other mineral-rich waters. It is cleansing, purifying and protective. It has a strong female energy, alchemists believed it to be the opposite of sulphur which was the male energy.

In European folk magic and Hoodoo (and other paths) it is common practice to sprinkle a pinch of salt in each corner of the room before starting any spell work.

Salt on its own is very protective but mix it with any kind of pepper – black, red or cayenne and you get a much stronger mix.

Salt Magical Properties:
Cleansing, purification, protection
Ruling planet – Earth
Element – Earth
Gender – Feminine

There are different types of salt, these are just some of them:

Table salt: This salt is usually highly refined. It is heavily ground and most of the impurities and trace minerals are removed. Some table salt has added anti caking agents so that it flows freely, iodine is sometimes added as well. Food-grade table salt is almost pure sodium chloride, 97% or higher.

Sea salt: Sea salt is made by evaporating sea water. Like table salt, it is mostly just sodium chloride. However, depending on where it is harvested and how it was processed, it usually does contain some amount of trace minerals like potassium, iron and zinc. The darker the sea salt, the higher its concentration of "impurities" and trace nutrients will be. However, keep in mind that due to the pollution of oceans, sea salt can also contain trace amounts of heavy metals, like lead.

Himalayan salt: Himalayan salt is harvested in Pakistan. It is mined from the Khewra Salt Mine, the second largest salt mine in the world. Himalayan salt often contains trace amounts of iron oxide (rust), which gives it a pink colour. It does contain small amounts of calcium, iron, potassium and magnesium. It also contains slightly lower amounts of sodium than regular salt.

Kosher salt: Kosher salt was originally used for religious purposes. Jewish law required blood to be extracted from meat before it was eaten. Kosher salt has a flaky, coarse structure that is particularly efficient at extracting the blood. The main difference between regular salt and kosher salt is the structure of the flakes which are quite large. There isn't much difference between table salt and kosher salt other than the size although kosher salt is less likely to contain anti caking agents or iodine.

Celtic Salt: Celtic salt is a type of salt that originally became popular in France. It has a greyish colour and contains a bit of water, which makes it quite moist. Celtic salt contains trace amounts of minerals and is a bit lower in sodium than plain table salt.

Black salt: Ritual or Witches' black salt is traditionally used in hoodoo and folk magic for protection and to dispel evil and negative energy. It is a combination of regular salt mixed with charcoal. You can make your own black salt very easily by mixing 2 parts salt with 1 part ash from your fire/fire pit or charcoal if you have some, you can even use black pepper in place of the ash/charcoal.

Black lava salt: Is black in colour and is simply sea salt that is blended with activated charcoal. You may see it labelled as Hawaiian Black Salt.

Indian black salt (or kala namak): An Indian volcanic rock salt. It is known by many names including *Himalayan black salt,* sulemani namak, and kala loon. It starts out as Himalayan pink salt or sodium chloride and is then heated to extremely high temperatures and mixed with Indian spices and herbs including the seeds of the harad fruit which contains sulphur. It also contains trace impurities of sulphates, sulphides, iron and magnesium which all contribute to the salt's colour, smell and taste.

Epsom salts: Epsom salts are not actually salt, but a naturally occurring pure mineral compound of magnesium and sulphate. Mix with essential oils or herbs to create bath salts. Use for beauty products, medicinal and relaxing baths, foot scrubs and cleaning - don't eat them.

Exercise: Experiment with different types of salt in your spell and ritual work. Keep a record of how each one performed and whether you notice a difference.

Graveyard Dirt

Graveyard dirt is exactly what it sounds like…it is dirt taken from a grave. Because of the source, and by source, I mean dirt taken from the grave of a dead person it has a habit of being used in hexes and curses. Does that make graveyard dirt dark magic? I think it depends on which grave the dirt came from and who is wielding the spell. It will also depend on what your own beliefs are about dealing with or connecting with the dead. There is no doubt either way that graveyard dirt carries a huge amount of magical power.

Personally, I love the peace and tranquillity that most graveyards have, and I like wandering around investigating. I have no qualms about collecting and using graveyard dirt although these days you do have to be careful that no one sees you collecting it, because being arrested for desecrating a grave is not high on my agenda. But...and here is the important part for me, you must know a bit about who resides in the grave you collect the dirt from. Dirt from the grave of a thief or a murderer is going to be fairly toxic. Dirt from a doctor or physician is going to have healing properties. Dirt from the grave of a soldier or service person is going to carry warrior energy – be careful who you choose.

You can if you wish just scoop up a handful of dirt from within the cemetery or graveyard boundaries, not necessarily from a specific grave. Or even collecting dirt and dust from gravestones rather than digging in an actual grave. This is a personal choice; you must do what works for you.

Some folklore suggests that 'real' graveyard dirt must be taken from just above the actual coffin and some state that three scoops must be collected: one from over the head, one from over the heart and one from below the feet of the body. Personally, I am not going to go to those lengths because that would definitely get me a night in the cells.

If all you need is a handful of graveyard dirt then you can just scoop it up and carefully pop it in a bag, if you need more you could take a pot plant to the grave and take home the earth that you dig out to put the plant in. I would suggest that you only do this on a relative or friend's grave – to avoid upsetting other people.

I like to get to know the spirit within the grave first, make a connection and ask permission and I also like to leave an offering. I think it is only good manners, because basically you are disturbing their peace. Coins or libations are traditional gifts in exchange for graveyard dirt.

So, what is graveyard dirt used for other than hexing? Well it actually has very strong protection properties.

Protection dirt: To protect your child as they leave your home pop a small amount of graveyard dirt on the back of your left hand, then as the child turns to go out the door throw the dirt over their head to bring in protection.

Success spell: Using nine handfuls of graveyard dirt, mix with salt, pepper and sulphur, then burn some of it on charcoal. As it burns visualise the success and goals that you wish to achieve. Repeat as and when necessary, as the power within this mixture lasts for a long time.

Exercise: If you fancy collecting some graveyard dirt, document where you obtained it from, what time of day, what time of year and then what you used it for and how well it worked.

Stones and Pebbles

You can find stones anywhere, it might be in the hedgerow, the forest, a field, on the seashore or in your garden, if you are really stuck then you can buy them in a bag at home depot stores.

Stones carry a huge amount of earth energy with them and they have all sorts of uses. If you are lucky enough to live by the sea or a river you may even find hag stones, sometimes called holey stones, hex stones or faery stones. Basically, they are stones where the water has worked through them and made a hole in the centre.

In folk lore hag stones were often used to ward against curses, nightmares, evil spirits and of course witches... They can also be used to look through to see into other worlds, realms or to see faeries. It is also said that you can look through the hole in a hag stone and see things in reality as it helps to look past any glamour or illusions.

These stones were used to keep away the evil hag spirit that would bring nightmares and so the stones were hung in bedrooms and placed on windowsills.

Some sailors would tie holey stones to the bows of their boats to protect against malevolent witchcraft. Similarly farm buildings would have a small holey stone or pebble tied to the key for the building – this was to prevent the witches that rode the hedgerows at night from hexing the farm and to prevent the witches from 'hag riding' the horses.

Wearing a hag stone around your neck as an amulet was said to protect the wearer against the evil eye and would also apparently prevent the wearer from being pixie led whilst out walking.

The holey stone was also said to be able to cure disease either by wearing the stone as a pendant around your neck or by rubbing the stone over a wound or painful joint.

I am assuming you don't want to use hag stones to protect against witches...they can be used for all sorts of protection and healing spell work. They can be worn as amulets or popped into medicine pouches or witches' bottles, you can also just put them on your windowsills or hang one above your doorway for protection. If you are looking for a bit of fertility, they are also good to hang over your bed to help facilitate pregnancy.

If you happen to find several hag stones, they can be strung on a piece of string, each one spaced apart and knotted below, this adds to the power of the stone bringing knot magic into play as well.

Hold a hag stone in your left hand and visualise success and your desires, rub your thumb around the hole in the stone in a deosil (clockwise) direction. Keep the stone with you and repeat the spell regularly to reinforce the magic.

But...depending on what area you live in hag stones aren't always easy to find so...use your intuition and pick pebbles or stones that appeal to you, sometimes a nice-looking stone will find its way to you. Each stone has the power of the element of earth so it can pack a good protection punch even if it hasn't got a hole in it.

If you have worries or troubles or feel that you need to get rid of some negative vibes, then send them into a pebble or stone. Once you have released your woes into the stone throw it into a river or the sea or bury it beneath the earth...taking your troubles away with it.

Flat pebbles can also be used to draw beautiful images on, I have several that I have used as god and goddess representations on my altar, I also mark the compass directions on large stones to use in ritual. You can draw images of animals on pebbles to use as animal spirit guide correspondences or just write positive affirmation words on pebbles to keep in the house to remind you to be happy.

If you manage to find a large flattish stone, it can be used as a garden altar or for burning loose incense upon.

Don't forget that a lot of buildings are created from stone too, whether it is natural sandstone, brick or concrete. They all have the element of earth running through them.

Exercise: Keep a note of any pebbles or stones you collect and where they came from, it might prove useful if you come to use them in a working because you then have some of their history and can use that as a base for any magic.

Sand

If the beach is a sandy one, then you have found yourself another magical ingredient. Sand is made up from tiny particles of rock and minerals. Where your location is, will depend on the exact composition but generally it is a mixture of silica in the form of quartz or calcium carbonate. Brilliant white sand might be made from limestone, coral and shells. The yellower sand may be from granite and onto the black or dark sand which is often from volcanic basalts.

Sand makes a very useful base to stand candles on to collect wax drips or keep an area safe from flame and it also does the same job in the base of a cauldron – health and safety conscious obviously.

To me sand also represents time and it can be used in magical workings for that intent. It can be added to medicine pouches and spell workings.

The sand is also representative of all the elements, the earth, the ocean, the wind and the sun.

Think about the beach and sitting on your sun lounger, shades on, cocktail in one hand and book in the other; a perfect ideal for relaxation, so sand can bring that intent along with it.

Sand is excellent to use for banishing things, bad habits or people – write the name of the person or the bad habit you want to get rid of in the sand and then either let the ocean waves wash it away or if you are at home you can pop some sand in a dish, write the name and then pour water over it to wipe it away.

Use sand to create your circle in ritual. Of course, sand already has salt built into it from the sea so you could use it in any magical way that you would use salt.

Either sitting on the sand or bringing some home with you and putting it in a flat tray you can use the sand as a blank canvas and draw whatever shapes you like. Use it as a meditative tool or create a spiral and follow it around with your finger for meditation.

Exercise: If you are able to collect any sand, make a note of where it came from and when and then document the results from any magical workings that you use it in.

Clay

The definition of clay is *'stiff, sticky fine-grained earth that can be moulded when wet, but when dried or baked turns solid'*. If you are a gardener then you will likely know the quality and type of your soil, mine is clay, quite thick clay. It does make gardening a challenge sometimes. However, clay can be used in magic in all sorts of useful ways and it represents the element of earth.

You might not want to use a lump of clay from your garden, but you can buy air dry clay from craft shops. The clay can be fashioned into deity symbols or statues, offering dishes or runes. It can also be used to mould around herbs or crystals to create a spell.

Herbs and Plants

Each plant has an association or correspondence with one of the elements. Often it is based upon the magical or medicinal properties of the plant. You can work with the plant in meditation or use the actual item as an ingredient in incense or spell work. Here is a basic list of plants and herbs that correspond to the element of earth to get you started:

Beech
Beech Magical Properties:
Wishes, creativity, spirituality, divination, luck, success
Ruling planet – Saturn
Sign – Sagittarius
Element – Air and Earth
Gender – Feminine

Cornflower (Batchelor's Buttons)
Cornflower/Batchelor's Buttons Magical Properties:
Love, psychic powers, protection, fertility, abundance, Faeries
Ruling planet – Venus, Saturn
Element – Water, Earth
Gender – Feminine

Cramp Bark
Cramp Bark Magical Properties:
Relaxing, meditation, stress, tension, anxiety, healing, rebirth, protection
Element – Earth
Gender – Feminine

Cypress
Cypress Magical Properties:
Release, binding, grief, protection, healing
Ruling planet – Saturn
Sign - Aquarius
Element – Earth
Gender – Feminine

Dogwood
Dogwood Magical Properties:
Loyalty, trust, faithful, protective
Element – Earth
Gender – Masculine

Echinacea
Echinacea Magical Properties:
Crone magic, power, healing, abundance
Ruling planet – Venus, Mars
Element – Earth
Gender – Feminine

Grass
Grass Magical Properties:
Protection, psychic powers, knot magic, abundance
Element - Earth

Honesty
Honesty Magical Properties:
Money, monsters, truth
Ruling planet – Moon
Element – Earth
Gender – Feminine

Honeysuckle
Honeysuckle Magical Properties:
Prosperity, psychic powers, protection, balance, lust, meditation, memory
Ruling planet – Jupiter
Sign – Gemini, Cancer
Element – Earth
Gender – Masculine

Horsetail
Horsetail Magical Properties:
Fertility, snakes, longevity, strength, cleansing
Ruling planet – Saturn
Element – Earth
Gender – Feminine

Ivy
Ivy Magical Properties:
Protection, healing, binding, love, abundance, fidelity
Ruling planet – Saturn, Moon
Sign - Scorpio
Element – Water
Gender – Feminine

Knotweed
Knotweed Magical Properties:
Binding, health, clarity, worries

Ruling planet – Saturn
Element – Earth
Gender – Feminine

Lungwort
Lungwort Magical Properties:
Healing, cleansing, releasing, calming
Ruling planet – Mercury
Sign – Taurus, Pisces
Element – Earth
Gender – Masculine

Magnolia
Magnolia Magical Properties:
Earth magic, fidelity
Ruling planet – Venus
Element – Earth
Gender – Feminine

Mugwort
Mugwort Magical Properties:
Strength, psychic powers, protection, dreams, healing, astral travel, feminine energy, cleansing
Ruling planet – Venus, Moon
Sign - Cancer
Element – Earth
Gender – Feminine

Patchouli
Patchouli Magical Properties:
Grounding, Earth magic, prosperity, money, protection, sex magic, balance, calm
Ruling planet – Saturn
Sign - Virgo

Element – Earth
Gender – Feminine

Plantain
Plantain Magical Properties:
Strength, protection, healing, energy, courage
Ruling planet – Venus
Sign - Capricorn
Element – Earth
Gender – Feminine

Primrose
Primrose Magical Properties:
Love, protection, faeries, changes, growth
Ruling planet – Venus
Element – Earth
Gender – Feminine

Sorrel
Sorrel Magical Properties:
Healing, health, love, grounding
Ruling planet - Venus
Sign – Capricorn, Taurus
Element – Earth
Gender – Feminine

Tulip
Tulip Magical Properties:
Love, peace, protection, prosperity
Ruling planet – Venus
Element – Earth
Gender – Feminine

Valerian
Valerian Magical Properties:
Protection, purification, love, sleep, peace, animal spirit, stress
Ruling planet – Venus, Jupiter
Sign - Virgo
Element – Water, Earth
Gender – Feminine

Vervain
Vervain Magical Properties:
Protection, love, purification, peace, sleep, healing, money, inspiration, shape shifting
Ruling planet – Venus
Sign - Gemini
Element – Earth
Gender – Feminine

Yew
Yew Magical Properties:
Death and rebirth, transformation, astral travel, ancient knowledge, knowledge
Ruling planet – Saturn, Mercury
Element – Water, Earth
Gender – Feminine

Roots

Most plant roots also correspond with the element of earth. The roots of a plant hold an immense amount of magical power and have a connection to earth magic as well, because they spend their entire life under the soil. The roots of most plants can be dried and used in any kind of spell work just as you would use the dried leaves or flowers but there are some that work particularly well from the root. As with any plant check first whether the roots are toxic or need to be handled with care.

Roots if they are big enough can also have symbols and sigils carved into them.

Nature Mandalas

Mandalas are easy and fun to make and are incredibly magical to work with. Use fallen petals, seeds, twigs, pebbles and leaves from the plants in your garden or pick those that you need (after asking permission from the plant) and make a mandala pattern on your lawn or patio. As you add each petal or leaf make your request, adding your intent and positive energy into the pattern you are creating. A mandala can also be created indoors using herbs, spices and ingredients from your kitchen cupboards.

Incense

Incense can be a loose mixture burnt on charcoal or by lighting incense cones and sticks. Incense is used to clear negative energy, create sacred space, complement spell work or add energy to a ritual. If you can't use incense for health reasons you could try using essential oil on a burner or scented candles. I often pop loose incense onto the top of an oil burner with a tea light underneath. The heat warms the blend and disperses the scent but doesn't give off any smoke. Incense is used frequently to cleanse, whether it is by passing the item through the smoke of the incense itself or by using incense to smudge something – your home, your body or an item. The power of the smoke cleanses and purifies. Loose incense can also be used in spell pouches and witch bottles but also to draw sigils or symbols with.

I start with a tree resin base such as frankincense or copal. Add in something woody to help it burn longer and then dried herbs and spices. To boost the scent, you can add a few drops of essential oil to the mixture.

Some earth element incense blends
Use equal parts of each ingredient.

Earth incense #1	Earth incense #2	Earth incense #3
Patchouli	Benzoin	Vervain
Mugwort	Primrose	Patchouli
Cypress	Cypress	Myrrh

Kyphi

Kyphi (kapet) is an ancient Egyptian incense blend burnt for use in ritual, healing and within the home. It was believed to be made from 'things that delight in the night'. Although recipes for a similar incense were also created in ancient Greece. It smells sweet, earthy and provocative.

The Egyptian word 'kapet' is believed to originally mean a substance that was used to clean and scent the air.

References to kyphi were made in some of the ancient pyramid texts. Often as one of the luxury items that a well to do Pharaoh could hope to find in the afterlife.

A lot of the earlier texts, although referring to this incense don't give any recipes. Later papyrus writings include the ingredients, the earliest being around 1500BC.

Writings during the time of Ramesses III include ingredients that were donated to the temples with the specific purpose of creating kyphi.

During the first century BC Plutarch visited Egypt and he describes the method of making this special incense, telling us that the ingredients were added one at a time as magical words were read out loud. He also suggests that kyphi was used as a drink to cleanse the body. The incense being specifically burnt at dusk each day in the temples.

Rufus of Ephesus included a recipe in his writings circa 50AD.

Circa 100AD Dioscorides wrote 'De Materia Medici' which contained a recipe for kyphi and recommended it be used as incense to purify temples and taken as a drink.

In the temple of Philae and the temple of Edfu you can find recipes for this incense inscribed on the walls.

A lot of the recipes seem to include raisins, wine and honey (yum) with a resin such as frankincense, myrrh and mastic. Adding in pine, grasses and often cinnamon, some also include mint, sweet flag, inektun, bitumen of Judea, cyperus, aspalathos, seseli, rush, lanathos, cardamom, peker and juniper berries. Some of the ingredients could be sourced locally however others would have had to be imported.

Later recipes can be found in Greece however they use less ingredients and are created in a much simpler fashion.

Preparation seems to vary although essentially the resins, grasses and spices are ground together, and any liquid drained off. Berries and kernels are ground to a fine powder and added in. A little wine is added to the combined mixture and left overnight. Raisins are soaked in wine and added, the mixture is then left for another five days. The complete mixture is then boiled until it has reduced considerably. Honey and frankincense are also boiled together until reduced then both mixtures are combined with myrrh then being added.

Simpler recipes mash the raisins, berries and wine together with the dry ingredients being ground together and mixed with honey then the mixture is combined.

It does seem quite a long-winded process to create but if you fancy the challenge there are plenty of recipes and methods on the internet, just google it. However, I have included an example recipe here, based on a recipe one of my lovely students discovered.

Kyphi incense recipe

5 raisins
1/2 teaspoon frankincense resin
1 tablespoon red wine
1/2 teaspoon benzoin resin
1 teaspoon sandalwood
1/4 teaspoon myrrh resin

1/4 teaspoon dried juniper berries
1/4 teaspoon dragon's blood
1/2 teaspoon honey
1/2 teaspoon cinnamon

Soak the raisins in red wine overnight.

Using a pestle and mortar, pound the sandalwood, juniper berries and cinnamon to a decent powder.

Now pound the frankincense, benzoin, myrrh and dragon's blood into small granules.

Mix the dry ingredients and resin granules together.

Drain the red wine from raisins and discard the liquid (sorry). Mash the raisins in a pestle and mortar. Add the raisins and honey to the dry mixture, mix thoroughly, then form into pea sized balls. Now spread the balls out on non-stick parchment for two weeks. They will need to be turned every few days to aid the drying process. Once cured store in a sealed bag or jar.

The balls can be burnt on charcoal discs or placed in the top of an oil burner over a tealight.

Exercise: Keep a note of any blends that you create and write up how each one worked. It is useful to keep a record for future blends.

Essential Oils

Essential oils have been used for thousands of years in religious ceremonies, for anointing, filling a room with fragrance, in foods and perfumes and for healing and well-being.

When purchasing essential oils do make sure they are pure and not mixed with chemicals or 'watered down'. Some of the oils can be expensive but remember that you only use a few drops at a time so they will last.

An essential oil is a concentrated essence of the plant. The oil is extracted from either the seeds, the peel, the resin, leaves, roots, bark or flowers.

Oil blends are useful for dressing candles for spell work, picking a corresponding oil to your intent and rubbing the candle with the oil. Or adding to your own bath water for a ritual bath or using to anoint yourself before ritual. Oil blends can also be added to an oil burner, I pop a piece of wax into the top first then add the oil, it stops it from burning. Please test a drop or two on a small area of your skin before you go slapping on loads of oil, just in case you are allergic to it. NEVER put essential oil straight onto your skin, always mix it into a base oil first.

A useful method for breathing in essential oils is to create your oil blend then add it to a jar containing a couple of tablespoons of coarse sea salt. Mix together and pop a lid on the jar. Then when you feel the need, open the jar and take a couple of deep breaths.

Oil blends are easy to make, and you can use any type of base oil such as almond oil, jojoba oil, apricot kernel oil, coconut oil, even olive oil. Then add a few drops of essential oil in whatever blends you want. If you are experimenting with blends, I would suggest using pieces of card to test the scent on first. Put a drop of each essential oil on a small slip of card (or paper towel) add the next oil and sniff to see if you like it, then add the next drop etc. Then you won't end up ruining a whole bottle of base oil by adding in random essential oils.

For a blend to use in an oil burner, bath or diffuser you can create a blend without using a base oil. Any blend you are intending to use on your skin for anointing or massage NEEDS to be diluted with a base oil. As a general rule of thumb, I would use 10ml of base oil to 20-25 drops of essential oil.

Some earth essential oil blends

Earth essential oil blend #1
4 parts patchouli
4 parts cypress

Earth essential oil blend #2
2 parts patchouli
2 parts vetiver
2 parts frankincense
2 parts cypress

Earth essential oil blend #3
4 parts patchouli
3 parts cypress
1 part vetiver

Earth essential oil blend #4
2 parts cypress
2 parts pine
3 parts magnolia

Exercise: Keep a note of any blends that you create and write up how each one worked. It is useful to keep a record for future blends.

Witch Bottles

Something I have made for years are witch bottles. I always keep a couple in the house and renew them regularly. I think of them as very much linked to the element of earth. Their purpose in my home is to soak up negative energy and keep the house full of happy positive vibes, which I very much associate with the element of earth. However, witch bottles can be made for any intent.

These are so easy to make; you don't need special pretty bottles; you can just use old clean jam jars. Generally speaking, the modern-day witch bottles are very similar to historical witch bottles in their basic structure, even though their intended purpose has changed. The most common purpose for constructing a witch bottle today is to capture negative energy and send it back out as positive.

Basically, a witch bottle is a container of some sort, usually a jar or a bottle, which is filled with objects that correspond to a given intent. The items are magically charged as they are added and can also be recharged with energy for as long as is needed, provided the bottle does not get broken.

Traditionally a witch bottle would have contained nails, earth, stones, knotted threads, herbs, spices, resin, flowers, candle wax, salt, vinegar, oil, coins, ashes and quite often urine.

Originally witch bottles were used to keep witches away. They also used to contain all sorts of bodily fluids, hair and fingernail clippings – you can add these if you want to.

Start with your jar or bottle, then as charge each item before you add it, layering up the 'ingredients' as you go.

It really is up to you what you put in. I like to put in three nails to attract negativity and for protection, I also put in a piece of string with three knots in, knotting in my intent with each tie. If it is for prosperity, I often drop in a silver coin. I usually put salt in for protection, cleansing and purification. I also like to add some kind of dried pulse – lentils or beans to 'soak' up any negative energies. Garlic is good for protection too. Then add any herbs, spices and flowers that correspond with your intent – rose petals for love, cinnamon for success, mint and basil for prosperity etc. Keep filling the jar or bottle up until you reach the top then put the lid on. If you are using a jam jar, I like to draw a pentacle on the lid. If I am using a bottle with a cork, I like to seal the cork lid with dripped wax.

If you are making the witch bottle for protection for your own home I like to put in a pebble from the garden, a couple of fallen leaves from the tree in my yard and a bit of cobweb from inside the house, it makes it all more personal and ties the bottle to the energies of the home.

Tree Magic

Each variety of tree has specific magical properties and you will find on closer inspection that each individual tree has its own unique personality. To discover what each tree means and what magical properties it can or is happy to share with you I suggest meeting each tree and asking. However, I have listed below a general guide for tree magic. You can use seeds, bark, twigs and leaves from a specific tree to bring the magical property they hold into your magical workings. Or just print off a picture of the tree to use as the basis of spell work. And of course, if the tree is happy to gift you a large enough twig you can use it to make a wand with.

Alder: Confidence, bravery, spiritual growth, spiritual protection and journeys.

Apple: Fertility, love, peace, joy and faerie magic.

Ash: Communication, mental abilities, wisdom, understanding, spiritual love, balance, protection and weather magic.

Beech: Divination, healing, wisdom, ancestors and desires.

Birch: Cleansing, rebirth, renewal, emotions, psychic protection, moon magic and new beginnings.

Cedar: Cleansing, protection and spirit work.

Cherry: Grounding, centring, stability, focus, intuition, divination, spirit work, healing, love and animal magic.

Elder: Banishing, protection, changes, healing and faerie magic.

Elm: Fertility, death and rebirth, goddess, grounding, focus and faerie magic.

Hawthorn: Psychic protection, creativity, confidence, purification, patience, insight, weather magic, Otherworld, banishing and faerie magic.

Hazel: Knowledge, creativity, love, change, wisdom, inspiration and magic of all kinds.

Holly: Strength, power, protection, purity, beauty and prosperity.

Ivy: Strength, spiritual growth, protection, determination and success.

Maple: Spiritual healing, travelling, knowledge, communication and abundance.

Oak: Truth, knowledge, protection, long life, healing, centring, grounding, focus, intuition, courage, prosperity and leadership.

Pine: Centring, focus, dragon magic, protection, truth, abundance, purification, fertility and healing.

Poplar: Divination, banishing, hope, rebirth and a general multi-purpose wood.

Vine: Faerie magic, happiness, rebirth, knowledge and spirituality.

Walnut: Astral travel, weather magic and motivation.

Willow: Death and rebirth, emotions, healing, love, divination and psychic work.

If you want to work with a tree on a one to one basis, i.e. the tree is physically right in front of you, approach slowly and see if you can send your thoughts out to the tree, ask if you have permission to come closer. Hopefully you will get a good positive feeling or even the whisper of acknowledgement in your head. If the energy feels hinky in anyway then just thank the tree and move onto another one.

Once you feel you have had permission slowly walk up to the tree and touch the bark with the palms of your hands, this helps you make a direct connection to the tree and the dryad/spirit within. If you have questions, need healing or just want to spend time with the tree then the best way is to sit beneath it with your back leaning against the trunk. Spend some time, talk, ask questions and most importantly listen. Trees are ancient and they carry a huge amount of knowledge and wisdom. Once you are finished, remember to thank the tree and if possible, leave an offering; just a splash of water is fine, but anything natural will work such as pebbles, shells and flowers.

Dryads and Tree Spirits
The belief that spirits (or ghosts as they were sometimes believed

to be) lived in trees goes back a long way, the Old Testament has references to sacred groves.

Celts, Romans and Egyptians amongst other cultures all believed in tree spirits.

If you look up the dictionary definition of the word 'dryad' it says: *"in folklore and Greek mythology – a nymph inhabiting a tree or wood"* which is just about spot on. Each tree will have its own inner spirit as all plants do, but tree spirits are specifically named dryads.

Greek mythology tells us of dryads, hamadryades and oreads – female nature spirits that dwell within trees, woodlands, groves and forests with a particular fondness for oak trees. All the texts and images from mythology seem to depict dryads as female.

A hamadryade is born with the tree and bound to it for the entire life span of the tree, when the tree dies so does the hamadryade.

Dryads can be found within their own tree or very close by as they never venture far from it. They are incredibly shy and if startled will quickly disappear into the tree.

In Celtic mythology you will find the same spirits but with different names such as tree nymphs, sidhe draoi or faerie druids. The world of Faerie is vast and there are many, many different types of fae associated with trees and woodlands.

Mythology and folklore have a huge number of stories and details for dryads and tree spirits, if you are interested it is a fascinating subject to do some research on.

Devas and Plant Spirits

Of course, if each tree has its very own spirit then it follows that every plant does too. And of course, each one is unique and has an individual character and personality. Plant spirits can be called upon to help with knowledge and guidance but particularly with healing. A spiritual journey can be undertaken to meet with a plant spirit to obtain healing. Each plant will offer a different and unique type of healing.

The word 'deva' may have originated in Persia and migrated to Greece and then onto the rest of Europe. The word 'deva' is Sanskrit and means 'shining one' and this may refer to the aura that is said to shine around the plant that you are working with. A deva is a plant guardian, but it also has other tasks such as healing plants, helping them grow and protecting and nurturing a whole area of plant life - basically they are nature's architects.

Exercise: Research your local area and find out what trees and plants grow in your locality. Make notes about each one with pictures or sketches of the leaves, flowers and seeds to help identify them. Re-visit at different times of the year to see and record the changes.

Sticks and Twigs

If you are looking for sticks or twigs to use, then I would recommend you look on the ground first rather than cut them direct from the tree. The trees usually provide enough twiggy gifts without the need for cutting. However, if you do need to cut a twig or small branch from a tree please do ask permission first, just let the tree know what you need it for and always cut cleanly, never rip it from the tree otherwise infection can set in.

Twigs can be made into all sorts of magical items from the obvious handmade wand to twig crafts or a fetish.

- Weave twigs into a crown or circlet and wear to impart the magical properties of the tree.
- Put hazel twigs on your windowsill to bring protection from storms to your house.
- Hang three hazel twigs tied together on the side of your house to protect against fire.
- Use small Y shaped branches for divination.

- Wearing ash bark is said to protect against powerful magic.
- If your child is poorly get them to climb through the split in the trunk of an ash tree to bring healing.
- Ash wood makes good broom handles and wands because of its strength and protective properties.
- Make an amulet from ash twigs to bring out the healing solar energy; tie two small ash twigs together into an equal arm cross, fasten in the centre with gold or yellow ribbon, charge the amulet in the sun.
- Carve a wish into a beech stick then bury it in the ground to make your wish come true.
- Use a wand made from beech wood to connect with spirit and the divine.
- Carry small pieces of beech bark with you for luck and success.
- Grind up a small piece of beech wood and pop the powder into your right shoe to bring good fortune.
- Use birch bark in protection spells.
- Birch twigs are traditionally used for making a witch's broom.
- Dry out pieces of birch bark and use them to write spells on.

Exercise: Make a note of any leaves, seeds or twigs that you collect, where they were found and what you used them for. Detail any magical workings and how well the results worked.

Magical Food

Just as each plant or herb has magical properties, so does food. Use them as offerings, eat to absorb the magic or use in spell working. Here are some foods that correspond to the element of earth:

Avocado
Avocado Magical Properties:

Beauty, passion, love, fertility
Ruling planet – Venus
Element – Earth
Gender – Feminine

Aubergine
Aubergine (Eggplant) Magical Properties:
Prosperity, wealth
Ruling planet – Jupiter
Element – Earth
Gender – Feminine

Barley
Barley Magical Properties:
Love, healing, grounding, protection
Ruling planet – Venus
Element – Earth
Gender – Feminine

Beetroot
Beetroot Magical Properties:
Passion, love, beauty, grounding
Ruling planet – Saturn
Element – Earth
Gender – Feminine

Blackberry
Blackberries Magical Properties:
Prosperity, protection, fertility, Faerie
Ruling planet – Venus
Element – Water, Fire, Earth
Gender – Feminine

Blueberry
Blueberries Magical Properties:
Calm, peace, protection, passion, fertility
Ruling planet – Moon
Element – Earth, water
Gender – Feminine

Brazil nut
Brazil nut Magical Properties:
Love, prosperity
Ruling planet – Venus
Element – Earth
Gender – Masculine

Bread
Bread Magical Properties:
Depends on the grain used, all breads are good for offerings
and grounding
Element – Earth
Gender – Feminine

Butter
Butter Magical Properties:
Peace, spirituality, Faerie
Ruling planet – Moon
Element – Earth
Gender – Feminine

Cake
Cake Magical Properties:
Happiness, ritual, rites of passage, offerings, celebration,
grounding
Element - Earth
Gender – Feminine

Cashew nut
Cashew Magical Properties:
Prosperity, energy
Ruling planet – Sun
Element – Fire, Earth
Gender – Feminine

Cheese
Cheese Magical Properties:
Success, happiness
Ruling planet –Saturn
Element – Earth, Air
Gender – Masculine

Corn/Cornmeal
Corn Magical Properties:
Abundance, luck, prosperity, offerings, fertility
Ruling planet – Sun
Element – Fire, Earth
Gender – Feminine

Eggs
Eggs Magical Properties:
Fertility, creation, life, new beginnings, divination
Element – Water, Earth, Air, Fire
Gender – Masculine/Feminine

Egg Shells
Cascarilla is made from eggshells that have been crushed and ground to a powder. It is used in hoodoo and folk magic as well as other magical practices. The powder can be dusted on the body to protect from spirit possession and acts as a shield from psychic or magical attack. It can be sprinkled around the perimeter of your home to create a peaceful environment and

to protect from intruders. It can also be used for drawing runes, sigils or other symbols in rituals and workings.

Egg Shell Magical Properties:

Protection, peace

Element – Earth

Gender – Masculine

Flour

Flour Magical Properties:

Various depending on the type of grain

Element – Earth

Game

Game Magical Properties:

Fidelity, divination, power, energy

Element – Fire, Air, Earth, Water

Gender – Masculine

Honey

Honey Magical Properties:

Happiness, healing, love, prosperity, passion, spirituality, faerie

Element – Water, Earth

Gender – Feminine

Kiwi fruit

Kiwi Fruit Magical Properties:

Love, romance

Ruling planet – Moon

Element – Water, Earth

Gender – Masculine

Liquorice

Liquorice Magical Properties:

Love, passion, balance
Ruling planet – Venus, Mercury
Element – Earth, Water
Gender – Feminine

Macadamia nut
Macadamia Magical Properties:
Prosperity
Ruling planet – Jupiter
Element – Earth
Gender – Masculine

Maple syrup
Maple Syrup Magical Properties:
Love, money, attraction, positive energy, healing, binding
Ruling planet – Jupiter
Element – Earth, Water
Gender – Masculine & Feminine

Mushroom
Mushrooms Magical Properties:
Strength, courage, magic, balance
Ruling planet – Moon
Element – Earth
Gender – Feminine

Oats
Oats Magical Properties:
Passion, fertility, prosperity
Ruling planet – Venus
Element – Earth
Gender – Feminine

Parsnip
Parsnip Magical Properties:
Male energy, sex magic
Element – Earth
Gender – Masculine

Pasta
Pasta Magical Properties:
Psychic powers, protection, communication, creativity
Ruling planet – Mercury
Element – Earth
Gender – Masculine

Peanut
Peanut Magical Properties:
Masculine energy, prosperity
Ruling planet – Jupiter
Element – Earth
Gender – Masculine

Pecan nuts
Pecan Magical Properties:
Prosperity
Ruling planet – Mercury
Element – Air, Earth
Gender – Masculine

Pistachio nuts
Pistachio Magical Properties:
Hex breaking, grounding, divination
Ruling planet – Mercury
Element – Earth, Air
Gender – Masculine

Pomegranate
Pomegranate Magical Properties:
Growth, fertility, wishes, death, rebirth, new beginnings
Ruling planet – Mercury
Element – Fire, Earth
Gender – Masculine

Potato
Potato Magical Properties:
Energy, magic, grounding, prosperity, healing
Ruling planet – Moon
Element – Earth
Gender – Feminine

Pumpkin
Pumpkin Magical Properties:
Prosperity, Crone magic, healing
Ruling planet – Moon
Element – Earth
Gender – Feminine

Quince
Quince Magical Properties:
Love, happiness, fidelity, protection
Ruling planet – Saturn
Element – Earth
Gender – Feminine

Raspberry
Raspberry Magical Properties:
Love, protection, strength
Ruling planet – Venus
Element – Water, Earth
Gender – Feminine

Rhubarb
Rhubarb Magical Properties:
Willpower, worry, love, protection
Ruling planet – Venus
Element – Earth
Gender – Feminine

Rice
Rice Magical Properties:
Prosperity, fertility, protection, rain, grounding, stability
Ruling planet – Sun
Element – Air, Earth
Gender – Masculine

Rye
Rye Magical Properties:
Love
Ruling planet – Venus
Element – Earth
Gender – Feminine

Salt
Salt Magical Properties:
Cleansing, purification, protection
Ruling planet – Earth
Element – Earth
Gender – Feminine

Sesame
Sesame Magical Properties:
Prosperity, protection, energy, strength, secrets
Ruling planet – Sun
Element – Fire, Earth
Gender – Masculine

Soya
Soya Bean Magical Properties:
Fertility, passion, prosperity, luck, psychic powers, spirituality
Ruling planet – Moon
Element – Earth
Gender – Feminine

Spinach
Spinach Magical Properties:
Passion, fertility, strength
Ruling planet – Jupiter
Element – Earth
Gender – Feminine

Strawberry
Strawberry Magical Properties:
Love, fertility, romance, luck, success
Ruling planet – Venus
Element – Water, Earth
Gender – Feminine

Sweet potato
Sweet Potato Magical Properties:
Love, passion
Ruling planet – Venus
Element – Earth, Water
Gender – Feminine

Turnip
Turnip Magical Properties:
Protection
Element – Earth
Gender – Masculine

Wheat
Wheat Magical Properties:
Prosperity, rebirth, abundance, wishes
Ruling planet – Venus
Element – Earth
Gender – Feminine

Wine
Wine Magical Properties:
Spirituality, offerings, happiness, love
Ruling planet – Sun (red wine), Moon (white wine)
Element – Earth, Fire
Gender – Masculine and Feminine

Exercise: Keep a record of which foods you use in magical workings and what the result was. It is useful to refer back to for future spells.

Earth Recipes

With cake in any form, bread, butter, eggs, flour and oats all coming under the element of earth you are spoilt for choice when it comes to baking! Here are a few of my favourites:

Parkin

Parkin is a traditional English cake, a gingerbread that contains oats. This recipe is thought to have come from the old pagan practice of baking oat and spice cakes to celebrate the beginning of winter. In Lancashire they were called Har Cakes after the Norse god Har, and in Derbyshire they were named Thor Cakes after the god Thor. Sometimes called 'tharve' cakes as they were cooked on the hearth.

225g/8 oz golden syrup
50g/1 ¾ oz black treacle
110g/4 oz butter

110g4 oz dark brown soft sugar
225g/8 oz oatmeal
110g/4 oz self-raising flour
2 teaspoons ground ginger
Pinch salt
1 large egg
1 tablespoon milk

Preheat the oven to 140C/275F/Gas 1.
Grease and line a 7"/18cm cake tin.
Pop the syrup, treacle, butter and sugar into a saucepan and melt over a gentle heat. Put the oatmeal, flour, pinch salt and ginger into a large bowl. Then pour the melted ingredients over. Mix together. Add the egg and the milk and stir to combine. Pour into the prepared tin and bake for about 1 1/1 hours.
Cool in the tin.

Peanut butter banana oatmeal cookies (vegan/GF)
I made these cookies for a recent ritual and they went down very well. They aren't too sweet and are not only vegan, but gluten free as well.

225g/2 cups oats
2 ripe bananas, mashed
125g/1/2 cup peanut butter (or other nut butter)
2 tablespoons maple syrup
1/2 teaspoon salt
1 teaspoon vanilla extract
45g/1/4 cup chocolate chips

Preheat the oven to 350F/180C/Gas 4.
Mash the bananas and add in the rest of the ingredients, mix well.

Drop spoonfuls of the cookie dough onto a baking sheet and flatten each one slightly.

Bake for 15 minutes.

Mead & blackberry cupcakes

Having picked up a bottle of half-finished mead I had the sudden thought that it might be lovely in a cupcake...as you do. This is the result. It is quite an alcoholic cake! I have used freeze dried blackberries in the frosting, but you could use fresh or frozen, just be careful of the moisture content. You can substitute the mead for cider or even apple juice if you prefer.

115g/1/2 cup unsalted butter softened
150g/2/3 cup granulated sugar
2 large eggs
1 teaspoon vanilla extract
236 ml/1 cup mead, cider or apple juice
300g/2 cups all-purpose flour
2 teaspoons baking powder
1 teaspoon ground cinnamon
1/2 teaspoon salt
Frosting
250g/8 oz butter
450g/16 oz icing (powdered) sugar
1 tablespoon ground freeze dried blackberries (or a handful of fresh/ frozen)

Preheat oven to 180C/350F/Gas 4 and line a 12-hole muffin tin with paper cases.

In a large bowl cream together the butter and sugar until light and fluffy. Add the eggs, vanilla, and mead and mix until fully incorporated.

Add flour, baking powder, cinnamon, and salt and mix until just combined.

Spoon the mixture into prepared muffin tin.

Bake for 20. Let cool completely.

To make the frosting whip together the butter and icing sugar until really light fluffy. Whisk in the blackberries. Ice your cakes.

Spiced chocolate bread pudding

I love bread pudding; it is one of my all-time favourites. I had a few left over hot cross buns...and decided to switch the recipe up a notch. If you don't have currant buns you could use any type of bun, bread roll or brioche roll.

225g/8 oz hot cross buns/currant buns
275ml/10 fl oz milk - for this recipe I used chocolate almond milk
50g/2 oz butter, melted
75g/3 oz soft brown sugar (use demerara or white if not available)
1 teaspoon mixed spice
1 egg, beaten
175g/6 oz dark chocolate chips
1 apple peeled and grated

Preheat oven to 180C/350F/Gas 4.

Line an oblong baking tray with baking parchment. 12 x 9 x 2 inches (approx. 31 x 23 x 5 cm) but the exact size is not crucial as long as the container is big enough for the mixture.

Either tear the bread into small pieces or blitz to make breadcrumbs depending on how smooth you want the finished pudding. Pour over the milk, stir and leave for about 30 minutes so the bread is well soaked.

Add the melted butter, sugar, mixed spice and beaten egg. Beat the mixture well until there are no lumps. Stir in the chocolate chips and grated apple.

Spoon into the baking tray.

Bake in the pre-heated oven for about 1¼-1½ hours.

Bakewell Tart

I have been looking at traditional British bakes and Bakewell tart must be one of the most recognised. The first recorded recipe for a Bakewell tart was in 1836 although variations have appeared since medieval times. The English town of Bakewell has a long history with creating a Bakewell Pudding although several other English places have a similar dessert (Buxton, Gloucester and Derbyshire for instance).

There are differences between the pudding and the tart. The pudding is made from puff pastry covered in a layer of strawberry jam and topped with a thick almond custard mixture. The tart is a shortcrust pastry case with a layer of strawberry jam and topped with a filling made from eggs, butter, ground almonds and almond essence. This is a raspberry version of a Bakewell tart...

For the pastry
200g/7 oz plain (all purpose) flour
1 tablespoon icing (powdered) sugar
125g/4.4 oz butter
1 egg yolk

For the filling
180g/6.3 oz butter, softened
180g/6.3 oz caster sugar
3 eggs
180g/6.3 oz ground almonds
1 teaspoon almond extract
200g/7 oz raspberry jam
25g/0.8 oz flaked almonds

Pop the flour and icing sugar into a bowl. Rub in the butter. Add the egg yolk and 2 teaspoons water and mix to a firm dough. Roll out onto a lightly floured board and use to line a deep 23cm loose-based, fluted tart tin. Chill for 15 mins. Heat the oven to gas 4/180°C/350C.

Bake the pastry case 'blind' for 15 mins. Remove the paper and baking beans and cook for a further 10 mins until the pastry is dry and a light golden colour. Remove from the oven and leave to cool.

For the filling, beat together the butter and sugar. Beat in the eggs, one at a time, then stir in the ground almonds and almond extract.

Spread the jam over the base of the pastry case. Spread the almond filling evenly on top, then sprinkle over the flaked almonds.

Bake for 35–40 mins until the frangipane filling is firm and golden brown on top.

Butterscotch Tart

This is a blast from the days of my school dinners...it was one of my favourites.

35g (1.2 oz) plain flour
175g (6 oz) butter
1 teaspoon vanilla extract
100ml (3 1/2 fl oz) milk
175g (6 oz) light brown sugar
1 pastry case (or make your own using the pastry from the previous Bakewell tart recipe)

Cube the butter and pop it in a pan with the sugar and milk. Heat over a medium to low heat until the butter has melted. Add the vanilla extract.

Slowly add in the flour, whisking as you do.

Heat for about five minutes, whisking constantly until the mixture has thickened.

Pour into a pastry case and put in the fridge to set. It will only take about an hour.

Crystals

Each crystal will have an association with one of the elements, sometimes more than one.

The basic fact is that crystals are taken from Mother Earth and some of the mining practices can be extremely harsh to the environment. Only you can make the decision about where you source your crystals from. There are some very good eco-friendly crystal providers, it may just take a bit of research on your part. A lot of crystal suppliers are now stating their sources which is very helpful. If you want to connect with the element of earth or use an earth crystal in your spell working, then these are some suggestions of crystals to use:

Agate (moss) magical properties

Nature, happiness, prosperity, wealth, longevity, friendship, success, abundance, healing, renewal, fertility, creativity, confidence, strength, love, beginnings, self-esteem, communication, emotions, stress, releasing, hope, trust, depression, growth, finances, cleansing, support, peace, stability, fears, luck, divination

Energy:	Receptive
Element:	Earth
Planet:	Moon

Bloodstone magical properties

Organisation, adaptability, anxiety, clarity, concentration, renewal, energy, self-confidence, connection, calm, protection, breaking barriers, selfishness, mysticism, insight, spirituality, truth, intuition, creativity, guidance, strength, healing, victory, wealth, money, power, invisibility, deception, negative energy, divine connection, past life, dreams.

Energy:	Projective
Element:	Fire, Earth
Planet:	Mars

Calcite (orange) magical properties

Amplification, energy, protection, grounding, centring, purification, peace, calm, emotions, balance, fear, depression, problems, power, potential, breaking patterns, changes, inspiration, creativity, positive energy, wealth, abundance, leadership, perseverance, finances, confidence, determination, money, opportunities, clarity, productivity, release.

Energy:	Receptive
Element:	Earth
Planet:	Sun

Chrysoprase magical properties

Courage, strength, wisdom, releasing, selfishness, imagination, happiness, success, balance, break barriers, protection, truth, healing, luck, prosperity, marriage, negative energy, transformation, love.

Energy:	Receptive
Element:	Earth
Planet:	Venus

Fluorite magical properties

Magic, imagination, discernment, aptitude, psychic protection, protection, purification, calming, relaxation, tension, anxiety, organisation, structure, challenges, declutter, releasing, support, breaking patterns, intuition, confidence, reassurance, comforting, communication, balance, spirituality, decisions, manifestation, peace, meditation, grounding, healing, cleansing, channelling, past life work, fairy realm, amplifying, memory, power, emotions, depression, stability.

Energy:	Projective
Element:	Water, Air
Planet:	Neptune

Goldstone magical properties

Ambition, luck, goals, determination, persistence, achievements, success, calm, emotions, energy, enthusiastic, confidence, self-belief, inner self, personal development, possibilities, courage, direction, clarity, uplifting, optimism, protection, deflects negative energy, knowledge, perception, manifestation, creativity, faith, energy flow, spirituality, abundance, wealth, grounding, perspective, ambition, drive, ingenuity, money, generosity, willpower, goals, emotions, divination (see also copper for additional magical properties).

Energy:	Receptive/Projective
Element:	Fire, Earth
Planet:	Jupiter, Venus

Hematite magical properties

Grounding, money, decisions, manifestation, finances, healing, focus, clarity, stability, protection, balance, divination, problem solving, emotions, self-esteem, productivity, doubt, anxiety, communication, strength.

Energy:	Projective
Element:	Fire, Earth
Planet:	Saturn

Howlite magical properties

Understanding, wisdom, connection, truth, meditation, focus, stress, anxiety, calm, strength, peace, releasing, emotions, selfishness, communication, creativity, inspiration, motivation, concentration, support, patience, relaxation, courage, past life work, astral travel.

Energy:	Projective
Element:	Earth
Planet:	Moon, Earth

Jasper (green) magical properties

Healing, sleep, emotions, empathy, compassion.

Energy:	Receptive
Element:	Earth
Planet:	Venus

Malachite magical properties

Changes, transformation, clarity, emotions, protection, support, healing, peace, travel, fears, growth, creativity, renewal, energy, wealth, money, opportunity, abundance, new beginnings, finances, success, business, focus, strength, wisdom, releasing, prosperity, breaking barriers, psychic abilities, manifestation, soothing, stress, love, power.

Energy:	Receptive
Element:	Earth
Planet:	Venus

Obsidian magical properties

Truth, healing, clarity, illusions, breaking barriers, integrity, grounding, centring, strength, courage, protection, cleansing, meditation, stress, calming, relaxation, depression, anxiety, wealth, luck, focus, emotions, power, determination, success, patience, perseverance, releasing, spirit work, spirituality, challenges, past life work, divination.

Energy:	Projective
Element:	Fire, Earth, Water
Planet:	Saturn, Jupiter

Pebble/hag stone magical properties

Protection, fairy magic, nightmares, dreams, healing, fertility, manifestation, negative energy.

Energy:	Projective
Element:	Earth, Water
Planet:	Earth

Petrified wood magical properties

Stability, grounding, calming, anxiety, fears, meditation, determination, decisions, strength, courage, patience, transformation, perseverance, success, luck, emotions, wisdom, past life work, insight, leadership.

Energy:	Receptive
Element:	Earth, Spirit
Planet:	Earth, Sun

Rose quartz magical properties

Love, happiness, emotions, spirituality, growth, fears, healing, sexuality, passion, calming, soothing, stress, depression, sleep, luck, wisdom, inspiration, success, intuition, grounding, balance, prosperity, self-esteem, harmony, trust, jealousy, gossip, beauty, peace, cleansing, fertility.

Energy:	Receptive

Element: Earth, Water
Planet: Venus, Moon

Smoky quartz magical properties

Grounding, centring, focus, negative energy, decisions, cooperation, creativity, emotions, depression, anxiety, jealousy, nature, protection, calming, manifestation, wishes, divination, meditation, insight, guidance, uplifting, fears, relaxation, releasing, abundance, luck, prosperity.

Energy: Receptive
Element: Earth
Planet: Saturn, Jupiter

Tiger's eye magical properties

Amplification, balance, harmony, releasing, fears, anxiety, courage, strength, self-confidence, focus, creativity, optimism, self-worth, protection, psychic abilities, healing, wealth, money, opportunity, abundance, prosperity, luck, success, commitment, determination, support, clarity, vitality, motivation, grounding, patience.

Energy: Projective
Element: Fire, Earth
Planet: Sun

Tourmaline (green/black) magical properties

Calming, harmony, balance, insight, spirituality, protection, negative energy, transformation, courage, grounding, fears, creativity, understanding, power, motivation, commitment, patience, stability, releasing, emotions, anxiety, strength, happiness, protection, relaxation, friendship, astral travel.

Energy: Receptive
Element: Earth

Planet: Venus, Mars

Turquoise magical properties

Purification, negative energy, protection, balance, relaxation, emotions, stress, spirituality, energy, depression, clarity, wisdom, understanding, psychic abilities, insight, intuition, past life work, communication, wealth, abundance, finances, prosperity, luck, decisions, friendship, uplifting, meditation, love, harmony.

Energy: Receptive
Element: Earth
Planet: Venus, Neptune

Exercise: Keep a record of your crystals and any experiences you have with them. Are there any that you found particularly linked to the element of earth?

Earth Animals

I love working with animal spirit guides. Each animal has a very unique energy and they can help and guide you, but also lend their characteristics to your spell work. Each animal has an element that they are associated with, it might be associated with their build, look, habits or where they live. Here are some suggestions for earth element animals:

Ant

Keywords: Hard work, teamwork, patience, determination, creating your dreams, community and equality.

Badger

Keywords: Wisdom, cunning, perseverance, earth magic, protection, creativity, fighting for your rights, organisation, fearless and solitary.

Bear

Keywords: Interactions, inner knowledge, introspection, intuition, dreamtime, renewal, moon and sun magic, opportunities, fearlessness and protection.

Boar

Keywords: Self-reliance, protection, warrior strength, spirituality, fierceness, nobility, strategy, personal power, re-birth, organisation, leadership, masculine energy, truth and transformation.

Chicken

Keywords: Fertility, sacrifice, rebirth, motherhood, nurturing, abundance, comfort, broodiness and fussing.

Cow/Bull

Keywords: Fertility, motherhood, sun and moon magic, stubbornness, insecurity, productive, earth magic, stability, aggression, defence, contentment and strength.

Deer/Stag

Keywords: Grace, reaching your goals, alertness, hunt, intuition, listening, transformation, observation, decisions, Otherworld, spirituality, messages, gentleness, innocence and adventure.

Dog

Keywords: Loyalty, devotion, protection, companion, faithful, hard work, communication, healing, support and warning.

Donkey

Keywords: Versatility, burdens, responsibilities, helping others, look after yourself, intuition, stubbornness and limitations.

Elephant

Keywords: Removing obstacles, strength, wisdom, confidence,

patience, learning, commitment, gentleness, compassion and support.

Fox

Keywords: Cunning, stealth, courage, observation, persistence, wisdom, magic, shape shifting and invisibility.

Goat

Keywords: Independence, strength, survival, foundations, security, growth, new pathways, confidence, stubbornness and direction.

Hedgehog

Keywords: Faerie, witchcraft, psychic abilities, prophecy, Otherworld, defence, challenges, calm, earth magic, abundance and fertility.

Horse

Keywords: Friendship, faithfulness, freedom, endurance, power, energy, travel, loyalty, overcoming obstacles, fertility and strength.

Mole

Keywords: Trust, senses, instincts, truth, guidance, Underworld, mysteries, faith and spirituality.

Monkey

Keywords: Honour, instinct, community, mobility, protection, playfulness, humour, compassion, understanding and communication.

Mouse

Keywords: Fertility, abundance, home, Underworld, death, cleanliness, industrious, ingenious, hoarding, reserves and behaviour.

Rabbit/Hare

Keywords: Fertility, seasons, moon magic, earth energy, intuition, emotions, reflection, social, community, jealousy, sensitivity, caution and joy.

Rat

Keywords: Spirituality, wisdom, fertility, wealth, cunning, resilience, cleanliness, sharing, kindness, helpful and resourceful.

Sheep

Keywords: Innocence, vulnerability, healing, dreams and inner work.

Snail

Keywords: Patience, protection, spiral of life, letting go of deadlines, slowing down, paying attention to details, inner work and withdrawal.

Squirrel

Keywords: Removing obstacles, solving problems, resourcefulness, preparing, planning ahead, balance, knowing when to rest, playful, action, communication and trust.

Wolf

Keywords: Teacher, pathways, guardian, understanding, new ideas, knowledge, wisdom, community, responsibilities, protection, sensitivity, intuition and truth.

Exercise: Keep an eye out for any animals that you see during your day. Not just outside, but also when reading a book, watching TV or adverts in magazines or on billboards. Take note of any animal images you might also see on fabrics, cushions or clothing. If you keep seeing the same one, it may have meaning for you.

Earth Animal meditation: Find a comfortable place where you won't be disturbed.

Take a few deep breaths, in and out...

As your world around you dissipates you find yourself standing on a stone floor, above you is a wooden roof and around you is a circular wall. Several wooden doors are set into the stone.

Each wooden door has a small window in the top, just about eye level.

Make your way to the first door and look through the window. Laid out before you is a densely packed forest, lush dark greenery, tall trees and fern covered floors.

Move to the next door and look through the window. You can see a dessert, white sand spread out as far as you can see.

Onwards to the next door, through the window you can see a freshly tilled field, furrows of dark brown soil edged with wild hedgerows.

The next door, this one looks out onto grassy green fields and hills, sprinkled with wildflowers.

Onwards, this time the window in the door shows you a tropical rain forest, with a tall canopy of palm trees strung with creepers and a floor filled with exotic plants.

And the last door, this one looks out to a farmyard, a muddy yard edged with gates into fields and several farm buildings.

Which one will you choose?

Pick one of the doors, open it and step into the scenery...

Call out and ask to be met by an earth animal.

Wait patiently and see what appears to you.

When an animal makes itself known, talk to it. Ask questions and listen carefully to any guidance given.

When you are ready, thank the animal for its time and advice.

Head back through the doorway.

Gently and slowly come back to this reality, remember what the animal told you. Open your eyes and wriggle your fingers and toes.

Exercise: Write down your earth animal experience, if you met a particular animal do some research on it.

Earth deities

Each deity is usually associated with one of the elements more than the others. Please do your research first. I would never recommend calling upon a god without knowing a proper amount of information about them first. Learn about their culture, myths and stories before you ask for their help. Here are some suggestions for deities that correspond with the element of earth, the list is only a start, there are a lot more. Quite often the earth element connection is agriculture, the harvest or the Underworld. I have only given brief descriptions, if any of them sing out to you, I encourage you to research and investigate further.

Abundantia

A Roman goddess of prosperity, fortune and overflowing riches, basically this girl is in the money – big time. Call on Abundantia for: Prosperity, luck, abundance, wealth and gambling.

Adonis

The Greek god of beauty and desire; he is also a god of vegetation and a fertility god. He is big on the hunting scene. Call on Adonis for: Glamour, passion, fertility, pleasure.

Athos

A mountain god hailing from Greece, possibly a son of the Earth Mother goddess, Gaia. Call on Athos for: Weather magic, strength, courage.

Arawn

A Welsh god, Lord of the Otherworld and a keen hunter. He is also very proficient in the art of shapeshifting. Call on Arawn for: Shapeshifting, hunting/seeking, Otherworld connection.

Ceres

An ancient Roman goddess of agriculture, grain and motherhood. A very kind and benevolent goddess she gifts mankind the harvest in return for cultivating the soil. Call on Ceres for: Grains, harvest, motherhood, fertile soil, cultivating the land, growing, food and compassion. (Equivalent to the Greek Demeter).

Cernunnos

An ancient Celtic horned god of the wild woods, nature and fertility. He also connects the three worlds. He is Lord of all animals. Call on Cernunnos for: Fertility, virility, tree magic, shape shifting, animal magic, Otherworld travel.

Dagda

The god of the Druids, master of the elements, of knowledge and a formidable warrior. The Dagda, or 'All-Father,' is the father of all Celtic deities, according to legend anyway. Dagda, pronounced 'DAH-dah,' protects his children and provides for them. Call on Dagda for: Wisdom, animal magic, warrior, fertility, protection, elemental magic, mental powers, creativity, sex magic, knowledge.

Demeter

An ancient Greek goddess of the harvest, grain and fertility. She is one of the Olympian gods. She has control over the seasons and whether, or not, the plants will grow. Call on Demeter for: Agriculture, seasons, grains, parenthood, growth, food, marriage, compassion and endurance. (Equivalent to the Roman Ceres).

Dionysus

Dionysus is an ancient Greek god of wine and the grape harvest. Basically, this guy likes a drink and a full-on party. I assume he often suffers from very bad hangovers... He was one of the twelve Olympians and a son of Zeus. (Equivalent to the Roman god Bacchus). Call on Dionysus for: Wild fun, wine making, fertility, ecstasy.

Gaia

Gaia is the primordial Mother Earth goddess of Greece. She is the first goddess, the creator of all life. She wields raw, maternal power. Call on Gaia for: All life and creation, the earth, the land, the sea, the mountains, fertility, motherhood and all greenery.

Geb

The ancient Egyptian god of the Earth. He is son of Shu the god of Air and Tefnut the goddess of moisture. With his sister (also his wife), Nut, the goddess of sky, they had four children, Osiris, Set, Isis and Nephthys. He is often depicted wearing a goose on his head (best not to ask), with green skin and plants growing from his body. Call on Geb for: Justice, creation, fertility, balance, wealth, harvest.

Hades

An ancient Greek god of the dead and King of the Underworld. He was married to Persephone whom he abducted, forcing her to remain in the Underworld for part of the year. (Equivalent to the Roman Pluto). Call on Hades for: Life and death, duality, wealth, fertility.

Horae, the

The Horae (or Hours) are ancient Greek goddesses of the seasons. They also cover justice and order. Thallo is the goddess of spring and protection for children. Auxo is the bringer of growth and

Carpo provides the food and harvest (autumn). A second group include Dike the goddess of justice, Eunomia goddess of order and law. And Eirene a goddess of peace and wealth. Call on the Horae for: Growth, protection, fertility, harvest, justice, order, law, peace, wealth.

Marduk

A Mesopotamian god, patron to the city of Babylon. Originally a god of thunderstorms he rose to a higher standing after conquering Tiamat (primeval chaos). He became Lord of the Gods of Heaven and Earth. He ruled over all nature and all people. Call on Marduk for: Fertility, nature magic, weather magic, strength, power.

Nephthys

An Egyptian goddess of the dead. Nephthys is the ancient Greek spelling of her name. In ancient Egypt she was Nebthwt which translates as 'Mistress of the house'. Basically, it means she ruled all of the house, the sky, the royal family and all of Egypt (don't mess with her...). She particularly protects the female head of any household. Call on Nephthys for: Shadows, darkness, secrets, death, protector of souls, Queen of the Underworld, magic and rebirth.

Osiris

An Egyptian god, Lord of the Underworld and Judge of the dead. His name translated means 'powerful' or 'mighty'. He is the first born of the gods Geb (Earth) and Nut (Sky). Call on Osiris for: Authority, beginnings, business, balance, change, cycles, life & death, enlightenment, fertility, goals, growth, wisdom, justice, marriage, the Otherworld, rebirth, renewal, success, transformation, trust, truth.

Pan

The part man, part goat ancient Greek god of the wilds, animals and trees. His father was Hermes and is mother was a dryad. The name Pan translates to mean 'all'. His name is also the basis for the word 'panic'. That should give you an idea about him, he is a little bit naughty... Call on Pan for: Music, hunting, fertility, fun.

Persephone

A Greek goddess of spring and Queen of the Underworld. Her story tells of the cycle of the seasons. She spends half the year above ground and the other half in the Underworld. Call on Persephone for: Spring, growth, happiness, agriculture, innocence, youth, Queen of the Underworld, keeper of souls, life, death, divination and magic. (Equivalent to the Roman Proserpina).

Pluto

An ancient Roman god, he rules the Underworld, whilst his brother Jupiter rules the sky and Neptune the sea. The Underworld doesn't just deal with the dead, it also contains a wealth of minerals and precious gems. He also owned a helmet of invisibility. (Equivalent to the Greek Hades). Call on Pluto for: Life and death, Underworld connection, wealth, invisibility, hidden truths.

Prithvi

Prithvi is a Hindu goddess of Earth. Her name literally translates from Sanskrit into the meaning 'earth'. She is believed to have created the world and all gods and men, along with her counterpart Dyaus. Call on Prithvi for: Nurturing, support, productivity, fertility, abundance.

Proserpina

A Roman goddess of spring and the Underworld. Her story relates to the changing of the seasons. Call on Proserpina for: Spring, maidenhood, growth, agriculture, earth, growth, the Underworld and keeper of ghosts. (Equivalent to the Greek Persephone).

Rhea

The Greek goddess of time and Titan mother of the Olympian gods. She also covers motherhood and female fertility. Her name translates as 'flow' and 'ease'. Call on Rhea for: Time, ancestors, calming, relieving chaos, menstruation, feminine energy and fertility.

Rhiannon

A Welsh goddess of patience and Great Queen of Wales. She is a moon goddess but also covers many other aspects. Call on Rhiannon for: Patience, the moon, compassion, enchantments, fertility, rebirth, wisdom, transformation, inspiration, dreams and guiding the souls of the dead.

Tammuz (Sumerian name Dumuzid)

Tammuz is a Mesopotamian god of fertility, new life and spring. Call on Tammuz for fertility, new beginnings, growth.

Earth deity meditation: Find a comfortable place where you won't be disturbed. Take a few deep breaths, in and out...

As your world around you dissipates you find yourself standing in a clearing in the centre of a dense forest.

All around you are trees and forest plants. Beneath your feet the floor is covered with a layer of leaves and ferns.

There is an opening in the canopy above you, through which you can see the dusky early evening sky.

Take a walk around the clearing and note all the different varieties of trees and plants. Touch the foliage and breathe in the scent.

In the centre there is a large flat stone so once you finish exploring your surroundings you make your way over and sit on the rock.

Sit quietly and listen.

You hear something making its way through the trees in front of you. At the moment you can only just make out the noise from the woods as they move through the undergrowth.

Then you start to see the shape of a person coming through the trees.

When they reach the edge of the clearing they step out and come over to you.

You are asked if they can sit with you.

Talk to them.

Ask questions.

Seek guidance.

Ask them their name, they may tell you, they may not.

Once they have finished, thank them for their advice.

The person gets up, turns and hands you a gift which you take with thanks. They head back into the forest and you watch them go until you cannot see them any longer.

Take a look at the gift, what were you given and why do you think they gave it to you?

Then when you are ready slowly come back to this reality, open your eyes and wriggle your fingers and toes.

Exercise: Do some research about the deity you met in your meditation. Find out the myths and stories. If you want to work with them further, you could even set up an altar dedicated to them.

Calling the Quarters

When in ritual most pagans will 'call in the quarters'. What does that mean? Well, we invite the four elements to join us and add their energy and qualities to the ritual. Each element corresponding to the four compass points. Earth being North of course. Some traditions choose to call in the Watchtowers or Guardians of the Watchtowers. The Guardians refer to the raw elementals and the

Watchtowers are the directions.

Earth Rituals

We probably all have our own way of working rituals. I have given my suggestion here but go with what works for you.

I have included quarter calls for all four elements because I like the balance and I think the elements support each other. However, you could just call upon the element of earth if you prefer.

I have given a ritual template here, use the deity list within this book for your gods and goddesses and also spell work to include, or add your own. I suggest you work a ritual for only one intent at a time, don't mix them up, it could confuse the energy.

Circle casting

Cast a circle to keep the positive energy raised within and to protect you from any negative outside influences. If you have the space you can walk the circle clockwise (to bring in energy) and perhaps sprinkle soil, salt or a corresponding earth herb or flower if you wish. If your space is limited, you can turn on the spot and visualise the circle. Make sure you 'see' the circle. Not only go around you but also above and below. You should end up with a visualised sphere or bubble around you. As you cast the circle you might like to add a chant such as:

I cast this circle round about
To keep unwanted energy out
Bringing in the element of earth
I cast this circle, my magic to birth
So mote it be!

Being a bit of a Star Trek fan, I tend to use the phrase 'make it so' rather than 'so mote it be'. You may prefer to use your own words.

Call in your quarters

Your options are to just turn and face each direction as you call them in. Or you might like to light a candle at each direction. You could use items such as lighting incense in the east, a candle in the south, a dish of water in the west and a dish of soil in the north. If space is lacking you could work with a shell for west, a pebble for earth, a feather for air and a match for south. As we are working with the element of earth specifically you may just want to place a pebble or some soil in the north and no items at all at the other points.

I start my quarter calls in the north, it seems to be the obvious compass point choice to me. A lot of witches and pagans start in the north. Although druids tend to begin their rituals by saluting the sun as it rises in the east. From the start point I turn clockwise. Give a call for each quarter, something like:

Element of earth
I invite you this ritual to tend
From the direction of North
Stability and grounding your energy to lend
Hail and welcome!

Element of air
I invite you this ritual to tend
From the direction of East
Intellect and wisdom your energy to lend
Hail and welcome!

Element of fire
I invite you this ritual to tend
From the direction of South
Passion and power your energy to lend
Hail and welcome!

Element of water
I invite you this ritual to tend
From the direction of West
Emotions and intuition your energy to lend
Hail and welcome!

Deity

It is entirely up to you whether you call upon deity or not. If you do, please make sure you do your research first. Not only would it be impolite to call upon a god that you don't know anything about, it could lend entirely the wrong energy to your ritual. Think about working a ritual for love and calling upon a war god...messy doesn't even begin to describe it.

Obviously, this book is all about the element of earth so I have suggested a list of earth deities, but you may be drawn in another direction. Trust your intuition but definitely do your homework too. I usually call upon a god and a goddess when working ritual, for me it brings a balance. But you don't have to, if you prefer to just call a god or a goddess then go for it. You may just prefer to call upon Mother Earth instead. Call in your deity with something like this:

I call upon the goddess Abundantia,
Asking that you bring your gifts of prosperity, luck and abundance to me
Hail and welcome

Basically, you call them by name and then ask them to bring whatever energy you need, so for Abundantia you would ask her to bring all the money stuff with her.

If you were performing a ritual with the intent of uncovering secrets, you might call upon Pluto with:

I call upon the god Pluto,

112

Asking that you show me the hidden truths
Hail and welcome

If it is fertility you are after, then Pan would be your man:

I call upon the god Pan
Asking that you bring me the gift of fertility
Hail and welcome

Spell work

Any ritual is created with a purpose, an intent in mind. What do you want to work this ritual for? Prosperity? Strength? Grounding? Whatever it might be, this is the point in the ritual when you work your spell or even just use a meditation. Check out the spells and meditations suggested within this book or work with your own.

To the feast and drink!

Once your spell work or meditation is done it is time for the feast! This really has double purpose. One is to celebrate with food and drink. A bit of a blessing in the form of 'may you never thirst' and 'may you never hunger'. Some of the food and drink is often sprinkled onto the earth if you are outside as a thank you to the gods and nature. Feasting also helps you to ground during the ritual, after any energy work has been done. It doesn't matter what you use to eat and drink. At our Kitchen Witch rituals, we always have cake, because that's how we roll. Often, I make cake that corresponds to the intent of the ritual, using particular ingredients and flavours to add to the will of the event. But you can use bread, sweets, fruits or biscuits. Mead or wine is a traditional ritual drink, but anything goes. At our rituals we often theme it, so we might have flavoured waters or herbals teas and in the cold, we have even had hot chocolate.

Now you close it all down in reverse...

Deity

Don't forget your manners, deity need to be thanked for attending the proceedings. It doesn't need to be fancy, just a simple one or two lines. *"I thank the god/goddess for lending your energy to the rite today. Hail and farewell"*. It really is that easy. But of course, you can add more text if you prefer.

Quarters

Next is thanking the elements in turn for their energy. Work in reverse order to that which you used initially. I start in the North when inviting the elements in, so I would now start with thanking water and working backwords to earth (North). Again, it doesn't need to be fancy, just something along the lines of: *"I thank the element of earth for being here today, hail and farewell"*. But I have made longer suggestions below:

Element of water
From the direction of West
Thank you for the energy you lent
Hail and farewell!

Element of fire
From the direction of South
Thank you for the energy you lent
Hail and farewell!

Element of air
From the direction of East
Thank you for the energy you lent
Hail and farewell!

Element of earth

From the direction of North
Thank you for the energy you lent
Hail and farewell!

Circle

Now the circle must be uncast. Walk widdershins (anti clockwise) around the circle and visualise the globe that you created, dispersing into the wind or back down into the soil.

I uncast this circle now the magic is all done
With my thanks for protection it gave
This circle is now open, but never broken
So mote it be!

Don't forget to give an offering to the earth if you didn't do so during the feasting.

Dispose of any leftover spell working items and/or candles.

Always leave the area clean and free from litter once you depart.

Earth spells

The element of earth aligns itself to several different intents, here are some of my suggestions for earth related spells. Follow them as I have laid them out or use them as a starting point to adjust with your own personal tweaks.

Egg and stone prosperity spell
You will need:

A pebble or small tumble stone crystal
An egg cup or small cup
A small bowl, slightly bigger than the egg cup
A second bowl, slightly larger than the other
A jug of water

If you work this spell on a Thursday, you will get an added abundance boost from the energy of Jupiter. Cast during a waxing moon phase to also ramp up the money vibe.

Set the largest bowl on a flat surface. Place the smaller bowl inside and then the egg cup inside that. Pop your pebble or crystal inside the egg cup. Pebbles carry the energy of the element of earth which is all about stability and material goodies. If you use a crystal, pick one that resonates with you, I like to use a green crystal for prosperity magic, but trust your intuition. Pour the water into the egg cup and keep pouring, allowing the water to overflow into the smaller bowl. Visualise money coming into you and all your financial needs being met as you do so. You might like to chant, something like:

Money, money come to me
Prosperity, abundance and financial security
Allow my cup to overflow
And my bank account, money to show
As is my will, make it so!

Keep pouring until the water overflows into the largest bowl. Say a little thank you and use the water in your garden or for pot plants. Pop the crystal/pebble into your purse or bag.

New month, new moon, new prosperity spell
You will need:

The new moon phase (most diaries have a note of this, but charts can be found online)
A white candle
Four green candles
A compass (or compass app on your phone)
A gold or silver coin

Working this spell on the new moon will add attraction and new sources of prosperity energy to your magic. The white candle represents you and 'the all'. Green uses colour magic to represent prosperity and money. The compass is used to find the directions but also symbolises your own direction in life. The coin does what is says…it represents money and prosperity. Tip: Use birthday cake candles, they are cheap and easy to source. If you can't find or don't have green candles, then white ones are a good 'multi-purpose' choice.

We will be working with the four compass directions; North, South, East and West these all have meaning:

North – finances, stability and material matters
East – intellect and inspiration
South – passion and energy
West – Emotions, intuition and releasing

Place your white candle in the centre of a safe level space. Use your compass (or compass app) to ascertain the four directions of North, South, East and West. Place a green candle at each of the four directions, in a square around the main white candle. Place the coin between the white candle and the green candle in the North. Light the white candle. Say this chant or one of your own, three times out loud. At the end of each chant turn the coin over.

Drawing magic from the new moon
Bring to me, fresh opportunities and new money soon
As I turn this gold coin around
Prosperity and financial security to me in abounds

Then starting with the green candle in the North, light all four saying at each direction:

New moon money arrive in from the North

New moon money blow in from the East
New moon money blast in from the South
New moon money wash in from the West

Sit quietly watching the flames and visualise money flowing to you and doors opening for new opportunities. Finish by saying *"make it so"*. Extinguish the candles and pop the coin in your purse.

House cleansing and blessing spell
You will need:

Vacuum cleaner or broom
1 teaspoon dried basil (to bring in the money)
1 teaspoon dried mint (for abundance)
10 tablespoons of bicarbonate soda

Pop the bicarbonate of soda into a dish. Hold the dried basil in your left hand and visualise cleansing and clearing of negative energy from your home to allow new money sources to come in then drop it into the bicarbonate of soda. Next hold the dried mint in your right hand and visualise positive and abundant energy filling every room in your house. Drop the mint into the bicarbonate of soda and mix together.

Starting at the top of your home, sprinkle a small amount of the mixture on your floors in each room, working your way down and through each room in your house. As you go you might like to chant:

Basil to clear away the old and make way for the new
Stagnant energy is released for money to arrive that's due
Add in magical mint to the stash
Abundant and positive energy along with the cash

Leave the mixture on the floors overnight if possible, but for at least an hour, then vacuum the carpets or sweep the floors to clear up. You might like to repeat the chant as you vacuum.

Egg magic

This is an easy method of working some magic to make your savings grow or to bring money your way. It isn't a quick fix for cash, but it will work slowly and surely to bring financial stability.

Take a raw egg and carefully write with a felt tip pen around the shell. You could just write one word such as 'money' or 'prosperity' but if you have small handwriting you might want to put 'bring money to me' or 'increase my bank balance'. Then bury the egg in your garden. If you don't have a garden the egg can be buried in some soil in a plant pot. As the egg breaks down it will not only feed the soil and the plants it will also bring prosperity your way. It works by using the symbolism of the egg as fertility but also bringing into play the four elements: earth for stability and material things, air for intellect and money wise ability, fire for energy and water for keeping emotions stable.

Balance your finances spell

This simple spell will help you balance your finances using simple natural items.

You will need:

A shell
A pebble
An elastic band or piece of string
Marker pen

The shell represents the element of water, this is the part of us that makes impulse buys based on our emotions and feelings. I bet we have all done that at some point! The pebble is for the element of earth, this covers finances, prosperity, grounding and stability. The element of earth puts our feet firmly back on the ground and brings a stability to our spending. Earth is also strongly associated with prosperity and the material things in life.

Using the pen draw a £/$ sign on the shell. Then draw another £/$ sign on the pebble. Hold one in each hand. Sit quietly and visualise yourself making sensible purchases. See your bank account nice and healthy and your savings account too. Paint a picture inside your head of you and your family being financially stable. Paying back loans and receiving extra money. It's your visualisation, let it take you where it needs to go.

When you are ready place the shell and the pebble together with the £/$ signs facing each other. Now wrap the elastic band or string around them both. Tying them together securely. The bonding of them together shows the universe that you are committed to being financially sensible and that you are worthy of receiving. As you bind them together say:

Element of water, bring my emotions and spending habits into
check
Element of earth, stability and security are now at my call and beck
The binding is now secure, let the magic flow
Make it so!

Place the shell and pebble where it can be seen regularly, on a bedside table or on a mantelpiece – this will remind you of the magic you have worked, and the commitment made.

Bucket and spade increase your finances, bury your debt spell

Oh, I do like to be beside the seaside...bucket and spade in hand you can do some creative sand magic to increase your finances or to bury those debts for good.

To increase your finances, you might like to get busy and build a sandcastle. All those millions of grains of sand represent complete and unending prosperity. Build castles and visualise each one adding to money to your bank account. Add in decorative shells and pebbles to add more magic. Visualise as you go.

Build your prosperity sand castles as far away from the waves as you can, the further away, the longer the abundance magic will last.

To remove your debts, you need to put that spade to work! Collect some shells and/or pebbles from the beach. Then set about digging a hole in the sand. Make it nice and deep. When the hole is ready take each pebble or shell and drop it into the bottom of the hole. As you drop each one, say out loud *"debt and money issues be gone"*. Drop as many pebbles or shells into the holes as you need to. Then start shovelling sand on top to fill the hole up. Once you are done say *"my debts are now buried and gone, bad finances are done"*. If you feel inspired to, you might like to jump on top of the sand or even do a little dance... Obviously, this magic needs some mundane back up, remember to think about the sand each time you are thinking about being frivolous with money...

Footprint money spell

Your feet connect you to the earth and the element of earth is all about stability, finances and worldly goods. Walking is also a useful tool, not only to get you from place to place but it moves energy as you go, it can carry that magic and make it work for you.

Using your feet to carry magic that brings prosperity and money your way.

Here are some suggestions:

- Pop a basil or mint leaf (both herbs being excellent for prosperity and abundance) inside your shoe.
- Make yourself a foot powder to dust the bottom of your feet or to sprinkle inside your shoes:
- 5 tablespoons arrowroot or cornflour

- 2 tablespoons of baking soda
- 3 tablespoons dried herbs – a mixture of ground cinnamon, mint and basil, ground finely
- Mix together and keep in an airtight jar.
- Draw a £/$ sign inside the bottom of each of your shoes, sandals of flip flops.
- Paint your toenails in a colour associated with money such as green, gold or orange. Paint one of your toes with a pound or dollar sign.
- Soil and sand both represent material things, take your shoes off and bury your toes in the earth of your garden or the sand on the beach and draw up the prosperity energy. Visualise that energy entering your feet. Then take nine steps, visualise money coming your way with each step. At the end of the ninth step say out loud 'make it so'. (Nine is a magical number, being three times three).

Harvest Sweeping

The broom or besom is a traditional symbol for sweeping out the old and bringing in the new. It is a feature of the hearth and home and all the good prosperity that it can bring. The act of sweeping is a natural gathering one.

You will need:

A broom, preferably a new one or make your own using a bundle of sticks tied together and fastened to a wooden pole.
Green ribbon (green is the colour for prosperity).
A small pouch
Dried mint
Dried basil
Dried grains – rice or barley work well

Take the pouch and add in the mint, saying:

As the Wheel turns and the first harvest is in
May this mint bring me money and prosperity within

Then add the basil, saying:

As the Wheel turns and the first harvest is in
May this basil bring me money and prosperity within

And finally add the grains, saying:

As the Wheel turns and the first harvest is in
May these grains bring me money and prosperity within

Take the green ribbon and tie the pouch onto the handle of the broom.

Now go outside of your front door and hold the broom in both hands. Spend a few moments visualising harvesting what you desire; money, prosperity, bills paid, items required, whatever it might be. See it all clearly in your mind.

Take the broom and start sweeping towards your door. You don't need to touch the ground with the broom (you don't want lots of dirt and dust being swept into your house) this is symbolic so keep the bristles just above the floor. Say:

As I sweep one, two, three
I sweep the harvest prosperity
As I sweep two, three, four
I bring abundance through my door

Repeat this chant three times and then go back inside. If you have the space, keep the broom in the heart of your home and use it regularly when you need money coming in.

Pumpkin prosperity magic

The tradition of carving pumpkins is an old one, although it began with carved turnips (which is a lot of hard work). They were used to frighten away evil spirits. However, the pumpkin with its bright orange skin brings success and with the amount of seeds inside it has a whole heap load of money energy. So, let's combine the pumpkin carving with some prosperity magic.

You will need:

A pumpkin
Carving tools
A clean jar

When you scoop out the seeds of your pumpkin, which is a really icky job! Save the seeds. Rinse them in cold water to get rid of the stringy pumpkin flesh and dry them on a tea towel. Spread the seeds over a large tray and leave them somewhere warm to dry out. When they are fully dry drop them into a clean jar, one or two at a time and chant:

Prosperity pumpkin seeds
Bring me money for my needs
As the seeds fill up the jar
Abundance from me will never be far

Pop the jar in your hallway or porch so that you will see it regularly. If you need a boost of cash, give the jar a shake.

There are many pumpkin designs, a lot of which have scary faces. And if you want to carve a face go right ahead but what about including a money symbol as well? A pound or dollar sign works well, carve it into the front and make it a feature of the pumpkin or just add a small symbol at the back. As you carve visualise money and prosperity coming your way.

Leaf magic

Leaves make a perfect item to use in spells and particularly for money magic. During the autumn fallen leaves are in abundance and they come in all shades of gorgeous colours. Find the largest fallen leaves that you can, whether it is from your garden or when you are out and about. This spell will help to increase your finances and reduce your debts.

You will need:

3 large fallen autumn leaves
Twine or string (natural)
A slip of paper
Pencil
6 cloves
Ground ginger

Take your largest autumn leaf and lay it out flat in front of you. Place 3 cloves in the centre and say:

With clove comes spice and heat, my debts now to retreat

Sprinkle a pinch of ground ginger on top and say:

Power and creativity with ginger come, money and abundance in a large sum

Now place the next leaf on top and repeat with the cloves and ginger. When you have your pile of leaves, cloves and ginger write on the slip of paper:

Money, prosperity and abundance come to me

Place the slip of paper on the top of your pile. Carefully roll the leaves up with the slip of paper inside and tie it securely with the twine or string. Your leaf parcel now needs to be buried. As you bury the parcel, repeat the chants:

With clove comes spice and heat, my debts now to retreat
Power and creativity with ginger come, money and abundance in
a large sum
Money, prosperity and abundance come to me

If a leaf is big enough it can be used to write wishes and petitions on that can be sent away on the winds, buried in the earth, dropped into running water or burnt in the fire.

Yule Tree magic

Most of us will be putting up a tree to decorate. It doesn't matter if it is a real pine or spruce or an imitation one. The important aspect is that it is a Yule tree. Green is an excellent prosperity and money colour. With the abundance of needles on a pine tree it also corresponds nicely with bringing in money. Add in the money magic by decorating with baubles and tinsel that represent wealth. Green and gold are perfect colours, silver works too and red adds a bit of power to it all.

You will need:

A Christmas tree (any size)
Lights
Baubles
Tinsel or other decorations

Once your tree is set up add your lights. Then you are ready. I like to bless my tree first. Stand in front of the tree and reach out your hand to touch the branches. Say:

With the blessings of the year
Let's get this abundance magic into gear

Festive fun and joy about
Let's give prosperity a shout

Now hold each ornament in your hands and visualise money and prosperity coming your way. You may even like to trace a pound or dollar sign with your finger into each item. As you hang each bauble, decoration or tinsel on the tree say:

Decorations shiny and bright
Bring wealth and prosperity to light
Money and abundance come to me
With the power of the festive Yule tree

Once your tree is fully decorated it should positively be singing with money magic energy.

A money magic garden

You could create areas in your garden that are specifically for prosperity and abundance. As each plant has one or more magical properties (usually several) you can grow plants as individual spells or create an entire bed with a specific intent. Seeds also work well as growing spells. Plant the seed with your intent and then add your energy to it each day to keep the spell going.

Prosperity garden

This might include lots of green foliage, green being a colour of money. Add in orange flowers for success and maybe plants that have lots of seeds such as fennel, seeds being good for prosperity. Grow plants that are associated with the magical correspondences of money and prosperity such as:

Ash, basil, bergamot (orange), calamus, camellia, cedar, chamomile, clover, comfrey, dill, dock, fenugreek, ginger, goldenrod, gorse, hazel, honeysuckle, honesty, jasmine, mandrake, mint, myrtle, nettle, oak, patchouli, periwinkle, poppy, skullcap, tulip, vervain and woodruff.

If you don't have room for a prosperity flower bed, then just plan a few pots specifically with prosperity plants in. If you don't have a garden, how about a pot plant on your windowsill with a prosperity magic plant in?

Add to the money magic by drawing £/$ signs on the plant pots or popping a silver coin in the soil before you plant the seeds or plants in the earth.

As you plant each one you could also chant:

With the element of earth as I plant
Money, wealth and prosperity I chant
Bring these things to me as the plants grow
Make it count, a really great big show

Employment pebble spell
This spell uses a pebble to help focus new job energy.
You will need:

A pebble, preferably one that you have collected yourself from a favourite place or you can use a crystal

Sit quietly and focus on the type of job you would like. Hold the stone up to your forehead, where your third eye is. Visualise yourself doing the job you would love, set the scene and walk through a day of work in your mind. See the interview, see it going well and then focus on the employer offering you the position.

Channel the positive energy, allow it to build and then flow from your forehead into the stone. The pebble is now charged with positive job energy. When you sit down to look through the paper or internet for a new job, pop the stone in front of you or hold it in your hand. If you need to write a letter for the position, place the stone on the paper as you write.

Once you get an interview don't forget to carry the stone with you in your pocket.

House protection spell

You don't need anything for this spell except your visualisation skills. Sit quietly and relax, preferably in the centre of your home. Connect with the earth energy from the ground beneath your house. Visualise a protective shield rising up from the soil, slowly and carefully enveloping your house. You can create a dome shape, a second skin around the house or even a pyramid over it. See the earth energy being supplied from below the ground. Once the house is enveloped, I like to say something like:

Protection of my home, stay safe whenever I roam

Stone home protection spell

You will need:

A small jar or pot
Pebbles

Using a small jar or pot, cleanse it with visualisation or incense smoke.

Take each pebble in your hand and bless it, saying something like:

In this pebble strength is bound
This spell will bring protection around

Pop the pebble into the jar or pot, repeat with as many pebbles as you need to fill the jar. Put the lid on and give a final blessing:

Element of earth in this pot

Bring protection to my home on this spot

The jar can be kept somewhere in the home or buried outside by the threshold.

Variation:

You will need four pebbles

Using the same pebble blessing as above, charge each stone

Bury one pebble at each of the four corners of your home

Bring peace tree spell

This spell uses tree magic to help heal a rift or sooth and argument between two people.

You will need:

A scarf or long piece of ribbon

Find a suitable tree whose trunk isn't too large, if the trunk splits into two then even better.

Take the scarf or ribbon and wrap it around the trunk (or split trunks). Walk around the tree nine times, widdershins (anti clockwise). Three times three is a powerfully magical number. As you walk say:

Friendship sits in lots of pain
Soothing and peace we need to gain

Now walk around the tree nine times, deosil (clockwise), as you walk say:

With peace and happiness now to be found
Friendships and love are now bound

Unwrap the scarf or ribbon and tie it around your wrist, wear it for a short while to remind yourself to forgive and make amends.

Don't forget to thank the tree.

Personal strength spell

This helps to give you strength for a particular situation.
You will need:

A dark coloured candle (purple, blue or brown)
White cotton/thread

Sit with the candle in front of you. Wind the cotton around the candle deosil (clockwise) three times, roughly about halfway down the candle. Then, take a few deep breaths in and out to calm and focus. Light the candle, focus on the flame. Now speak out loud, ask for strength to deal with whatever situation or issue you need to address. It doesn't have to be fancy, say it straight and in your own words. Allow the candle to burn down to the cotton.

Then bury or dispose of the rest of the candle.

Money pebbles

I am guessing that we all have a pebble or two in our gardens. Or we can find them when we are out and about. Pebbles align with the element of earth which is all about stability, material things and prosperity. Just sitting outside in the fresh air, the pebbles also soak up energy from the sun. The sun brings power, positive energy, growth and happiness. The humble pebble is a serious magical item. If you can find pebbles that have a flat surface, they are perfect to write symbols on, which is what we are going to do with this spell.

You will need:

Four pebbles, large enough to write a symbol on
Marker pens, in various colours if possible (or acrylic paint works well too)

Wash and dry your pebbles. Lay them out in front of you. Take the first pebble and draw a £/$ sign on the top with your pen or paint. Say:

With the magical element of earth
Symbol of money to bring what it's worth
Add in mighty power of the sun
Work your magic until it is done

You can just draw a simple £/$ sign or add in colour and design around it. Maybe a green leaf design to symbolize money growing? Then repeat with each of the other three pebbles. Draw the same design on each or mix it up a bit and use other signs or something else that represents money, prosperity and wealth to you. Say the chant as you work on each one.

When you have all four pebbles finished you will need to place them around your home. Try and get them in each of the four corners of your house. Just pop them on the floor in the corner of the room. Or you might like to place them outside, one either side of your front door to help money come in and then the other two at the back of the house. Placement will depend on the layout of your abode. But try and get them spaced out in a square. Once all four are in place, say:

With the placement of all four
Money come to me and more
Magic of the earthy stone
Make my house a money zone
Make it so!

Leave the pebbles in place and watch the money flow in!

Spell stone

If you find a particularly unusual stone or have one from a favourite place it can be used as a spell stone. I have one from Tintagel in Cornwall. Cleanse the stone by washing it and then purifying with incense or visualisation.

The stone can then be charged with your intent to use it as your own personal magical spell stone. When you are in need of working some magic, write your wish on a slip of paper. Fold it up and then place the spell stone on top. Keep it there until the magic has worked.

Releasing spell

You will need:

A pebble

This has got to be one of the simplest spells to let go of negative emotions or feelings. It can also be used to rid yourself of bad habits or cut ties from an unhappy situation. Take the pebble in your hand and allow all the negative emotions to drain from you into the pebble. Then throw it away. It could be into a river or the ocean or may be just into your trash can. The pebble could also be buried in the soil (away from your property).

Colour magic

I love to work with colour magic. It brings its own energy to spells and rituals. Bringing in a colour to represent an element can help not only boost your magic but help you to connect with that element.

Earth is often represented by the colour green or brown. Both of those work for me. If I was working magic for abundance or prosperity, I would bring in green as the colour of money. For stability or grounding, I would work with brown. However, go with what works for you. Black or yellow are also sometimes used. But if you live in an area with red soil you might prefer to work with red. Or perhaps a different colour or shade to represent earth for each season. Black for winter, yellow for spring, green for summer and orange for autumn would be my suggestion. I have listed below my idea for earth colours, I have included red although I associate it more with fire and yellow although I associate that more with air, but they also cross over into earth.

Earth colours

Black - protection, ward negativity, remove hexes, spirit contact, truth, remove discord or confusion and binding for spell work.

Brown – endurance, houses & homes, uncertainties, influence friendships.

Green – earth elemental, nature magic, luck, fertility, healing, balance, courage, work, prosperity, changing directions or attitudes.

Orange – the God, strength, healing, attracting things, vitality, adaptability, luck, encouragement, clearing the mind, justice, career goals, legal matters, selling, action, ambition, general success.

Red – fire elemental, strength, power, energy, health, vigour, enthusiasm, courage, passion, sexuality, vibrancy, survival, driving force.

Yellow – air elemental, divination, clairvoyance, mental alertness, intellect, memory, prosperity, learning, changes, harmony, creativity, self-promotion.

Earth divination

Divination forms often associated with the element of earth are tarot, runes and the ogham. Tarot, runes or ogham can be used to work spells or meditate specifically with the element of earth in mind.

Tarot

The whole pentacle/discs/coins suit in particular within tarot is very earth based as are all the Pages across the deck. Within the major arcana we have The Empress, The Hierophant, The Hermit, The Devil and The Universe all corresponding to the element of earth.

Runes

Rune sets are often made from wood, stone or crystals. Runes are found carved in stone across the globe. Inguz, uruz, wunjo, jera, berkana, ehwaz and othila rune symbols all particularly correspond with the element of earth. You can easily make a set of runes using discs of wood or smooth pebbles.

Ogham

Ogham sets are usually made from pieces of wood, as each one aligns with a particular tree, these seem perfectly aligned with the element of earth.

Geomancy

Geomancy is a form of divination that interprets markings on the ground or by throwing handfuls of soil or rocks.

Flower divination

You can make lovely pendulums with flower or seed heads, just tie one onto the end of a piece of thread and use it as you would with any pendulum. Flowers can also be used to 'cast' in divination. You can do this using either a plain piece of cloth or a large bowl filled with water. Gather together a selection of flower petals, heads and leaves. You will need to work out what flower part represents what, so a red rose petal might indicate love and a sage leaf might mean wishes etc. Once you have decided what each of your plant parts mean you can think of a question then cast the flowers onto your cloth or into the bowl of water. Where they land, what direction they land in, what other flower parts they land next to all will mean something – you will need to work out what.

Exercise: Work with some of the earth divination methods. See which one works best for you and what sort of results you get.

Astrology

For those of you that work with horoscopes, sun signs and moon signs. The twelve signs of the zodiac are split into the four elements. What we generally think of as our zodiac sign is the sun sign, we were born under. We usually take on a lot of the characteristics that the sign corresponds with, although we will also be affected by the moon sign we were born under as well. And of course, if you are working magic you can take into account the sign that the sun or moon is in to help boost your magic, which is what I am looking at here…

The earth signs are:

Taurus

Sign of fixed earth and the bull, which helps describe the attributes of those born under Taurus!

Ruling planet: Venus

Taurus (Apr 20th – May 20th) – ruled by Venus so it is all about beauty and love, patience, organisation, support, romance, careful, dedication, stubborn, lazy, vain, over cautious, stability, over indulgent and a 'lil bit on the cheap side.

Qualities: Stubbornness, productive, stable, practical, possessions, acquisitions, building, strong willed, hardworking, sensuous, artistic, magnetic, beneficent, musical, literary, persistence, security, pleasure, caution, reliability, solid goals, determination, romance, kindness, creativity.

Symbol: The head and horns of a bull, a circle of potential topped by a crescent of receptivity.

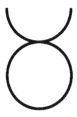

Virgo

Sign of the mutable (liable to change) earth. The scales of justice, the goddess Astrea who became the virgin maiden constellation, Virgo.

Ruling planet: Mercury

Virgo (Aug 23rd – Sep 22nd) – Ruled by Mercury and communication, dedication, hardworking, practical, humour, resourceful, self-destruction, uptight, critical and a tendency to have self-pity parties.

Qualities: Critical, eye for detail, operation, practical, discerning, intelligent, healing, craftsman, purity, analysis, service, perfection, observation, communication, insight, self-improvement, clarity, concentration, focus, consideration, organisation.

Symbol: The letter M with a closed loop. Represents the female genitals.

Capricorn

Sign of the cardinal fire (momentum, change). The goat or the god of nature, Pan.

Ruling planet: Saturn

Capricorn (Dec 22nd – Jan 19th) – ruled by Saturn a planet of discipline (sit up straight) and maturity, loyalty, family, hard work, devotion, honesty, no fear, pessimism, no forgiveness, cold, materialistic, fairly hopeless and frankly sometimes a bit of a snob.

Qualities: Materialist, achievements, responsibility, restraint, secrets, persistence, patience, aspirations, idealism, practical, hardworking, discipline, industrious, resourceful, ambition, conscientious, productivity, maturity, goals, strategies, self-discipline, control, security, tradition, structure

Symbol: The mountain goat with horns or a goat/fish hybrid.

Exercise: Create some magical workings using the energy of the earth zodiac signs. Try using them on the corresponding date. What were your results and experiences?

Saving Planet Earth

As Pagans, are we more concerned about the state of the planet? Can we do more? I suspect that being as in touch with nature as we are, we perhaps feel it very strongly – humans have infested planet Earth and done as much as we possibly can to destroy her. Mother Nature is suffering.

So, what can we do? My answer to that question is – as much or as little as you are able to. Even tiny baby steps towards helping out are important. Very few people have the resources or the bank balance to make a huge change in lifestyle, but we can make smaller changes.

I am a working wife and mother that has to feed hungry teenagers and a dog, my food bill is huge so I am restricted to how much I can do with that. In an ideal world I would love to purchase all organic meat, but my budget just doesn't stretch that far, but I do try and stick with farm assured. I don't have a local greengrocer, but I do have a vegetable box delivery service that is not far away, and they deliver big boxes of fabulous fruit and veg every week that has been grown locally. There is also no plastic involved and the boxes are reused. When I cook, I try to use up leftovers as much as possible, my mum did it with her cooking when we were kids – roast dinner on a Sunday, cold meat and potatoes on Monday and rissoles made with the last bits on Tuesday. One joint of meat lasted us three days! We don't seem to think like that so much these days, everything is disposable, and we waste so much food it is criminal.

And for pagans that use herbs and plants for magical purpose, think about where they are sourced from. I grow as much as I can in my garden. I don't order exotic and unusual ingredients that have to be shipped across the globe. Not only is that costly to me, but also to the environment. Smudging your home or working magic with herbs from a different continent surely cannot be as good as something you have grown in your own garden or that has been sourced locally? For me, it is all about connections – connections to the land that you live on and the area local to you. My magical ingredients come from my garden or my kitchen cupboard and as much as possible, locally sourced. Obviously, there are some things that don't grow in a suburban garden in the UK, cinnamon for instance is a personal favourite, but I am not about to grow a cinnamon tree in my tiny city garden! I must be realistic and can only do as much as I feasibly can. But every little helps.

My council has a recycling scheme, although they are a bit selective with what they take. We also pay a little each month to have a compost bin collection, for all our garden waste.

Recently I have looked at the amount of plastic we use in the house. Small changes have been made; shampoo bottles are being phased out and replaced with shampoo bars, which I actually love. Good old-fashioned bars of soap and natural body scrubs (in recyclable pots) in place of shower gel. Hand pump soaps at the sink are now soap dishes with handmade soap bars in. Small changes, that don't cost the world but will make a difference.

This week we discovered our washing up bowl had a crack in. Ah, I will replace that...and then I realised it was a huge lump of plastic that would be thrown into the world rubbish tip. My next thought was "why do we need a plastic washing up bowl when we have a perfectly good stainless-steel sink underneath it with a plug!" ... So, I won't be replacing that.

I love clothes...but the majority of mine come from charity shops or eBay. I love buying second hand because you get interesting finds that are much cheaper and help the environment.

My garden is tiny, but I cram as many bee, bird and insect friendly plants in as I can. I also provide bird seed and water for both the birds and the bees. In the summer months the noise of the bees is deafening.

Our car boot is full of long-life shopping bags that we use each time we do a supermarket shop. When I go out on a short trip, I take my wicker basket (much to the embarrassment of my youngest child...). I also take a fold up tote bag as well. All little gestures, but ones that mean I don't have to purchase plastic carrier bags in the shops.

With a household of five, I do a laundry load pretty much every day. It is frightening how much laundry detergent goes down the drain and into the water system. I have experimented with other options – soap nuts worked well at first, but after a few weeks the washing didn't seem to be as clean as I would like. I am looking into other options. During the dry days I hang the washing on the line, but during wet and wintery days I do use the tumble dryer. I have to, otherwise I just can't get through all the laundry. However, I stopped using tumble dryer sheets a while ago. I tested wool tumble dryer balls, but I didn't get on with them. Now I use reusable energy saving tumble dryer balls – and they are brilliant. No need for tumble dryer sheets and they shorten the drying time.

We also have a lot of washing up and we were getting through a washing up sponge a week, that's 52 plastic sponges a year going into landfill or the ocean. So, I researched…and now we have reusable dish clothes that can be thrown in the washing machine each week and last forever, without being replaced.

Just do it - Individually each of these is a small step, a little change that costs nothing or very little. But add it all up and it comes to quite an impressive list. We probably all do more than we think. Just make small changes, even if you only do one thing it will help.

We are all in this together, and together we can make a difference.

Earth Blessing

Along with all the practical things we can do to help heal Mother Earth I think it also helps to send her some healing every so often and to thank her for all that she does.

It doesn't have to be a long ceremonial or complicated affair. Keep it simple.

Light a candle in her honour and sit quietly visualising healing energy going down into the surface of the Earth.

Give an offering to the soil; water, wine, breadcrumbs or whatever you feel drawn to give. Send a blessing in her name.

If you work with Reiki or healing energy send some out to the Universe to dish out to anyone that needs it.

Sit outside and connect with the energy in your garden or your local park. Ask what you can do to help make things better for the planet.

We only have the one planet and it provides us with all that we need to live, laugh and love.

Let us remember to take care of it.

**MOON
BOOKS**

PAGANISM & SHAMANISM

What is Paganism? A religion, a spirituality, an alternative
belief system, nature worship? You can find support for all these
definitions (and many more) in dictionaries, encyclopaedias, and
text books of religion, but subscribe to any one and the truth will
evade you. Above all Paganism is a creative pursuit, an encounter
with reality, an exploration of meaning and an expression of the
soul. Druids, Heathens, Wiccans and others, all contribute their
insights and literary riches to the Pagan tradition. Moon Books
invites you to begin or to deepen your own encounter, right here,
right now.
If you have enjoyed this book, why not tell other readers by
posting a review on your preferred book site.

Recent bestsellers from Moon Books are:

Journey to the Dark Goddess
How to Return to Your Soul
Jane Meredith
Discover the powerful secrets of the Dark Goddess and
transform your depression, grief and pain into healing
and integration.
Paperback: 978-1-84694-677-6 ebook: 978-1-78099-223-5

Shamanic Reiki
Expanded Ways of Working with Universal Life Force Energy
Llyn Roberts, Robert Levy
Shamanism and Reiki are each powerful ways of healing; together,
their power multiplies. *Shamanic Reiki* introduces techniques to
help healers and Reiki practitioners tap ancient healing wisdom.
Paperback: 978-1-84694-037-8 ebook: 978-1-84694-650-9

Pagan Portals – The Awen Alone
Walking the Path of the Solitary Druid
Joanna van der Hoeven
An introductory guide for the solitary Druid, *The Awen Alone* will
accompany you as you explore, and seek out your own place
within the natural world.
Paperback: 978-1-78279-547-6 ebook: 978-1-78279-546-9

A Kitchen Witch's World of Magical Herbs & Plants
Rachel Patterson
A journey into the magical world of herbs and plants, filled with
magical uses, folklore, history and practical magic. By popular
writer, blogger and kitchen witch, Tansy Firedragon.
Paperback: 978-1-78279-621-3 ebook: 978-1-78279-620-6

Medicine for the Soul
The Complete Book of Shamanic Healing
Ross Heaven
All you will ever need to know about shamanic healing and how to
become your own shaman...
Paperback: 978-1-78099-419-2 ebook: 978-1-78099-420-8

Shaman Pathways – The Druid Shaman
Exploring the Celtic Otherworld
Danu Forest
A practical guide to Celtic shamanism with exercises and
techniques as well as traditional lore for exploring the Celtic
Otherworld.
Paperback: 978-1-78099-615-8 ebook: 978-1-78099-616-5

Traditional Witchcraft for the Woods and Forests
A Witch's Guide to the Woodland with Guided Meditations and
Pathworking
Mélusine Draco
A Witch's guide to walking alone in the woods, with guided
meditations and pathworking.
Paperback: 978-1-84694-803-9 ebook: 978-1-84694-804-6

Wild Earth, Wild Soul
A Manual for an Ecstatic Culture
Bill Pfeiffer
Imagine a nature-based culture so alive and so connected,
spreading like wildfire. This book is the first flame...
Paperback: 978-1-78099-187-0 ebook: 978-1-78099-188-7

Naming the Goddess
Trevor Greenfield
Naming the Goddess is written by over eighty adherents and
scholars of Goddess and Goddess Spirituality.
Paperback: 978-1-78279-476-9 ebook: 978-1-78279-475-2

Shapeshifting into Higher Consciousness
Heal and Transform Yourself and Our World with Ancient
Shamanic and Modern Methods
Llyn Roberts
Ancient and modern methods that you can use every day to
transform yourself and make a positive difference in the world.
Paperback: 978-1-84694-843-5 ebook: 978-1-84694-844-2

Readers of ebooks can buy or view any of these bestsellers by
clicking on the live link in the title. Most titles are published in
paperback and as an ebook. Paperbacks are available in traditional
bookshops. Both print and ebook formats are available online.

Find more titles and sign up to our readers' newsletter at
http://www.johnhuntpublishing.com/paganism
Follow us on Facebook at https://www.facebook.com/MoonBooks
and Twitter at https://twitter.com/MoonBooksJHP

You might also enjoy…

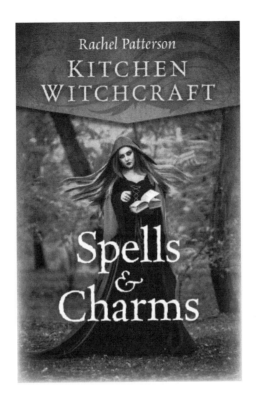

Kitchen Witchcraft
Spells & Charms

978-1-78535-768-8 (Paperback)
978-1-78535-769-5 (ebook)

You might also enjoy…

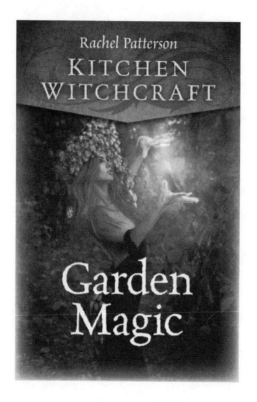

Kitchen Witchcraft
Garden Magic

978-1-78535-766-4 (Paperback)
978-1-78535-767-1 (ebook)

You might also enjoy…

Kitchen Witchcraft
Crystal Magic

978-1-78904-216-0 (Paperback)
978-1-78904-217-7 (ebook)